Sparkle and Shine

In a Dark and Dreary World

Dorothy Hill Gates

Sparkle and Shine

Copyright © 2017 by Dorothy Hill Gates

All Scripture is used from the KJV

Cover photo and author photo credit @ie_photographs
Makeup by Hannah Page

ISBN-13: 978-1974612833

ISBN-10: 197461283X

Printed in the United States of America

Dedication

To all my sweet sisters in Christ who want to sparkle and shine with confidence but are scared to let their lights shine. May this book be the spark to ignite the flame that is shining deep within. May you find the courage and the confidence to be a radiant light. May you use your light for the glory of God and allow your spark to reach others.

To Lora Shaner, Jenny Hill, Tori Porter, and Tammie Polk who helped edit, prayed, and encouraged me in this journey.

Thank you Jillian Martin for capturing my vision perfectly on the book cover photo. Thank you for all the time and effort spent behind the camera and behind your computer. You are priceless!

Thank you sweet Hannah Page for the flawless makeup, I felt beautiful and confident. You are so talented; can you do my makeup everyday?

To my precious husband who is my constant support and rock. I could never follow my heart's desires without your love and encouragement.

Table of Contents

Introduction

Isaiah 60:1- 2b

"Arise, shine: for thy light is come and the glory of the Lord is risen upon thee.

....the Lord shall arise upon thee, and his glory shall be seen upon thee."

How can we as Christians shine for the glory of God? We live in a day where Christians are now the enemy. We are looked upon as the crazy bad guy who encourages hate and non-tolerance. We are thought of as small minded, judgmental people who do not care about individuals.

Not so long ago, there was a respect and a reverence toward Christians, now there is disgust and distrust upon the mere mention of the word. The name Christian has been tainted and marred. We wonder how we can rise above the destruction, break through the darkness, and continue to sparkle? How can we shine our light in a dark world, when the world constantly rejects us and our Light?

I pray this study will answer these questions and encourage all of us to be the light that God has called us to be. I pray it will inspire us to speak truth in a loving compassionate way and share Christ boldly and unapologetically with others. May our voices be full of hope and not hate! Might we take a stand without stomping others into the ground! I pray this book will challenge us to Sparkle and Shine in a Dark and Dreary world, for the glory of God. Loving others the way God loves us.

Chapter One

This Little Light of Mine

I have a very simple mind and anytime I think of letting my light shine, I can't stop this simple mind of mine from automatically going to the well known children's song, *This Little Light of Mine.* Yep, that's my brain. Please tell me I am not alone and you thought of this song too. The words in this song are simple, catchy, and powerful. So, for the fun of it, let's sing it together.

THIS LITTLE LIGHT OF MINE
I'M GONNA LET IT SHINE
THIS LITTLE LIGHT OF MINE
I'M GONNA LET IT SHINE
LET IT SHINE
LET IT SHINE
LET IT SHINE

How amazing is the message in this short, simple song! We, as Christians, have a light and it needs to shine. In Matthew 5:14a we see that the Bible says, *"Ye are the light of the world..."* God tells us that our light is the light that the world needs and depends on. God calls you and me to be a light.

You may be reading this and wondering what is this light? How do I let it shine? Why does my light even matter? I am not a preacher, a missionary, or even a Sunday school teacher! Well, I'm so glad you asked, because your light is very important. Your light is your influence, your testimony, and your legacy. Basically, your light is the positive effect that you have on those around you. In the verse above we see that God said, *"YE are the light."* Yes, that's you! A lot of times, we think it is someone else's job to follow God and shine, but in this verse He calls you and He calls me. You might be thinking, "Why me?" Because, God knows that as a Christian there are people in your life that only you can reach, or be a ray of sunshine to. There is an influence you can offer to your circle of friends that no one else can offer. Your life can touch them in ways you never thought possible. God called you to be their light, to love them, to help them, and to encourage them.

We each have our own special light. It is unique and different from anyone else's light. Our lights will be seen and used in significantly distinct ways. How exciting and refreshing is this? I don't have to live my life in comparison to your life and vise versa. I can be unique and still be valuable to God, because my light is mine and your light is yours.

But know that this light cannot be lit in our own strength or power. It's a flame that only God can ignite deep in our hearts. The flame He starts will burn forever. Over time it might get a little dull and need to be rekindled but the magnificent truth is that it will never burn out!

John 8:12 has always been a favorite verse of mine. I remember learning it as a song at youth camp and it stuck in my head for life. *"...I am the light of the world: he that followeth me shall not walk in darkness, but shall have the light of life."* We each have a light and we each have a choice. What we choose to do with our light matters to the cause of Christ. I don't know about you but I want to follow Him with my whole heart and have a light that shines bright for Him.

Again, my simple mind is instantly drawn back to our popular children's song, but it's the next verse that is dancing around in my simple head. So, get your pointer finger up in the air and get ready to sing the next verse!!

HIDE IT UNDER A BUSHEL?
NO!
I'M GONNA LET IT SHINE
HIDE IT UNDER A BUSHEL?
NO!
I'M GONNA LET IT SHINE
LET IT SHINE
LET IT SHINE
LET IT SHINE

Again, what a powerful thought packed into that short simple verse. God does not want us to hide our light or be ashamed of our light. We see in the latter part of Matthew 5:14 "...*A city that is set on a hill cannot be hid.*" He wants us to let it shine bright for the entire world to see, just like a city sitting way up high on a hill.

Have you ever been for a drive through the country side and while enjoying the views and taking in the beautiful sights, you see a house sitting high on a hill? There it sits snug and cozy in the protection of the trees that are nestled around it. It looks so quaint and inviting and it has a way of drawing your attention to it. You can't help but notice the spectacular view it offers, almost as if it demands you to look its way.

This is what God is saying to us. Be a spectacular sight that demands the world's attention in a beautiful, positive, captivating way. You can use your influence to reach others! Think of the people God has put in your realm. Think of the ways God wants you to impact them for His Glory. Your light should shine in the most brilliant, radiant way so that others want what you have. You should draw people to God and not away from Him. Your testimony should be so effective that there is no doubt you love and serve the one true living God!

We must not hide our light, be ashamed of our light, or try to ignore our light. We were called to go and share it. We can not stay in the safe, protected bubble of our family, church, or circle of friends. We can not keep our light to ourselves. No, God has called us into this darkened world to spread His light. So, where has God called you? Who does He want you to share your light with? Who is it that you can reach or make a difference to?

I recently heard a quote by an amazing lady named Jill Briscoe. This incredible Saint of God has been on every continent of the world spreading and sharing the gospel. Her testimony is challenging and this quote inspired me so much that I had to share it with you. *"The orbit of your life and the area between your own two feet is your mission field."* Did I mention she is 83 and still travels, speaks, and serves God?

God may not call you to a foreign land to do mission

work, but He has called you to do a mission work where you are! Where is that? Could it be in your community, your neighborhood, your job? The people in your path are the ones God wants you to start with. Go, spread your light. Don't hide it, don't keep it to yourself, and don't ignore it. God gave us His Light so we may sparkle and shine to bring glory back to Him. Just let that light shine.

So how do we let our light shine?

1. By knowing and spending time with the One who gives the light

You can not share something you do not have. You can not fake it or pretend to have it. In order to let your light shine, you must know the Giver of the light and you must spend time with Him. There are no substitutes or shortcuts for having a relationship with Him. If you desire for your light to effectively shine for Him, then you must spend time with Him. This comes through reading your Bible, praying, obeying, and worshiping Him.

2 By investing in others and making a difference in those around you

I remember hearing the statement "*Love people not things*" over and over during my college years. It stuck in my head and was tattooed into my heart. To truly make a difference in other people's lives, we have to be more concerned about them than in our piggy banks, our schedules, our plans, and our routines. This is not easy, but let me tell you, it is truly more blessed to give. Whether it is your time, your money, your desires, or your prayers; you will be more blessed when you give! If you are going to impact the life of someone, you must invest in them. Who is God calling you to invest in? Is it your neighbor, co-worker, an acquaintance, a dear friend, the stranger at the grocery store, the new lady sitting in your church? Look around you, who has God put in your path? Pray and ask God to show you who you can shine your light to.

3. By being real

Don't be someone or something you're not. You may feel you are not worthy to invest in someone else. You may feel unqualified or unworthy, but please remember that someone needs you and they need you to be you. You don't have to be a Bible scholar, a preacher, or a Sunday school teacher to be used of God. Just be you, be real, and be genuine. The world is full of fake Christians and honestly, people are sick of them. God will use you the way you are. He is not looking for a super Christian; He is looking for a willing Christian! Be you and see what He can do through you.

4. By getting out of your bubble and your comfort zone

There is no way you can help, minister, comfort, invest, pray, love, or provide for others if your world revolves around you. I know it is hard to get out of your own bubble when life has a way of keeping you busy. But in order to let your life shine, you must get out of your bubble and look at others. There is a mission field everywhere you look, but you must slow down and look.

I get teased a lot by my family and friends because everywhere I go, I somehow end up talking to strangers. Whether it is at the grocery store, a restaurant, a gas station, the park, or even the bathroom (truth) I somehow strike up a conversation with people and before I know it, I know their entire life story. This may be aggravating to some, but to me it's a blessing. I feel that if I can be a little bit of Jesus to them in those few short (or long) moments, then I am shining my light. We get so busy being busy, that we forget to be kind to others around us. Maybe if we slowed down, smiled, sincerely compliment people, and encouraged them, we could share our lights in a positive way. You may have to step out of your comfort zone, but is that asking too much?

I John 1:7 *"But if we walk in the light, as he is in the light, we have fellowship one with another..."* Get out of your bubble and your comfort zone and learn to love the people around you.

5. Don't brag about what you have done

God may ask you to make some sacrifices or do some pretty incredible things. He may use you to bless others or provide a need for someone. When He does, don't fall into the trap of bragging on yourself. Let your good works speak for themselves and let others brag on you, then allow God to reward you for your obedience.

Proverbs 27:2
"Let another man praise thee, and not thine own mouth; a stranger, and not thine own lips."

Matthew 6:2-4
"Therefore when thou doest thine alms, do not sound a trumpet before thee, as the hypocrites do in the synagogues and in the streets, that they may have glory of men. Verily I say unto you, They have their reward. But when thou doest alms, let not thy left hand know what thy right hand doeth: That thine alms may be in secret: and thy Father which seeth in secret himself shall reward thee openly."

In the Bible times, an alm was money, food, or other donations given to the poor or needy; anything given as charity. So, we see here in Matthew that any time we are doing something out of charity or love we should not do it for the glory of men, but for the glory of God.

Don't forfeit your eternal reward for temporary praise.

Matthew 5: 16
"Let your light so shine before men, that they may see your good works, and glorify your Father which is in heaven."

This is what it is all about; shining the light that God has given us, so that we might bring glory back to Him. It's not about us or what we have done, it's all about Him. So, will you choose to shine your light? Are you willing to let God use you? Are you ready to sparkle and shine for the glory of God? My prayer is that you are willing and ready to take this imperfect journey to follow God where He leads you, to courageously let your light shine, and to lovingly invest in others so we may point them to Jesus.

Chapter Two

Be Who You Were Created to Be!

The year is 1991. It's all about big hair, big jewelry, big attitude, and big fun; and this 13 year old girl wanted to be right in the middle of it all. I was all about babysitting, roller-skating, slumber parties, hanging out with friends at the mall, and of course, boys! I loved dancing around to The New Kids on the Block and I faithfully watched every episode of Saved by the Bell and Full House. I soon found myself fascinated with one of the actresses and before long; I tried to be just like her. I got a perm, teased my bangs sky high, poofed my sides out to look like wings and I probably used a can of Aqua Net aerosol hairspray every week. I styled my hair just like this adorable actress. I tried hard to dress like her, act like her, and look like her. She was pretty, she was smart, she was witty, she had amazing hair, stylish clothes, a perfect TV family, a great circle of friends, a smile that would light up a room, and everyone adored her. So, if I could be just like her, then everyone would adore me too, right?

So, with my best efforts, I tried, and I tried hard to be just like her. I worked diligently to get rid of me and get more of her. So much so, that people began to tell me that I looked like her and this is what I had dreamed of! The more people told me I looked like her, the harder I would try to be her. Until one day, the cold facts of reality came crashing down on me hard, very hard.

During this particular summer, this insecure girl, who was desperately trying to be someone else, was at a youth conference in Texas. The conference had rented out the local skating rink and bowling alley. There were hundreds of teens scattered all about the buildings and parking lots. The majority of kids were skating or bowling, some were playing video games, and others were just content hanging out at the concessions. I remember, for some reason, I was all alone at this particular moment and I was feeling a little shy and overwhelmed by the huge crowd. I tried to force myself to go and skate. I loved skating and was a pretty confident skater. I was walking to the counter to pick up some skates (this was way before roller-blades) when suddenly, a group of boys (very cute boys) walked right up to me and started talking. They were all smiling nervously and acting a little shy. At first, I thought it must be some kind of a prank or a dare. But they kept talking and smiling and were actually acting very fascinated by me. Finally, one of the boys asked me if they could take their picture with me. WOW! I must be having a really good hair day because a group of boys, (really cute boys) wanted their picture with me! A smile as big as Texas broke out across my face! I shook my head yes, (because the words wouldn't come out of my mouth). My head began to swell as I thought about how cute I must be looking, but before my head could swell too big, another boy asked if he could have my autograph and held up a napkin. It was at this point that I got totally confused. Why would anyone want my autograph?

"Do What?" The words stumbled from my mouth in confusion.

"Well, you are that girl from TV aren't you?" another boy piped in, asking a little too loudly.

"Oh! Um, no." I stammered very embarrassed as nearby teens turned and looked in my direction.

"Sure you are! I would know you anywhere." He challenged back.

They were all looking at me eagerly, waiting for me to confirm that they were indeed standing in front of a beautiful, famous Hollywood actress. Instead, I shook my head *"No"*. They looked at me like I had a tree growing out of my nose.

"Oh, I get it," one of the other boys piped in, *"you don't want anyone to know you're here. You don't want everyone to bother you. It's okay, we won't tell anyone, but can we still get your autograph and your picture?"*

Again several of them held up a napkin for me to sign. I just happened to notice the music blaring loudly in the background, but somehow between that and the voices of hundreds of teens talking and having fun; it didn't seem to be loud enough to hide the sound of my heart pounding in my chest. These boys honestly thought I was a famous teenager, and just for a moment, I thought about playing along and pretending to be her. I thought about how glamorous it would be to sign these cute boy's napkins and take pictures with them. I thought about telling one simple lie, nodding my head *"YES"* and living out the dream. I mean, it wouldn't hurt anyone. How cool would it be to be popular, adored, and sought out by fans? And then there was the fact that these cute boys (really cute boys) wanted to get their picture with me. I mean, I could pretend to be her, get pictures with these guys, maybe get an address, or phone number of a few of them (this is what people did before there was social media haha) and maybe, just maybe…maybe what? How could I even think about pretending to be her? It would be a lie, it would only be pretend and the fantasy would not last!.

Then the truth hit me like a ton of bricks, and all too soon the devastating reality came crashing down on me. They did not want me; they wanted her, the girl I was trying to be. Fantasy was suddenly replaced with a hard dose of reality when one of the boys called me by the actress's name. It snapped me back down to earth. I knew then that the truth was they were only interested because they thought I was famous. And that hurt. I knew I had to end this charade quickly, it took a bit more convincing but when I finally got them to realize I was not a famous Hollywood actress, but just a simple country farm girl from Louisiana, I could see disappointment written all over their faces. They slumped their shoulders, crumpled up their napkins and shoved them deep down into their pockets. The looks of fascination and adoration were quickly replaced with displeasure and disinterest. They put their cameras down and quickly walked away.

There I was left standing alone with my shame, embarrassment, and my insecurities. Alone, feeling like a liar, a phony, and a fraud. I felt like I did not measure up, and as hard as it was, I learned a very important lesson that day. The truth was, I didn't measure up, nor would I ever measure up trying to be someone else. The simple truth was God had not created me to be that beautiful famous actress; He created me to be Dorothy Fawn Hill. He made me unique and one of a kind. He desired for me to embrace who I was. He wanted me to let my light shine for Him. He longed to use me for His purpose and bring glory to Him. But, He could not use me until I was ready to be me.

I had spent so much of my time trying to cover up those specific designs and qualities that made me Dorothy. I thought I was discovering who I was by being someone else. The reality of this scenario was that I was only losing myself, not discovering myself. I could never be my best while trying to be someone else. I could only be second best at being her, because, her life was already taken. But my life was there, ready to be lived, waiting on me to live it.

God makes no mistakes. You and I were designed for a unique purpose and a specific calling. There are people only you can reach and be a lighthouse to. These people need you to be real and authentic; they need you to be you. There are so many fake people out there, let's not be one of them. Be real and show the world the real you.

You may have a loud boisterous personality and feel you need to calm down. Or perhaps you are shy and timid and groups intimidate you, but you wish you could be the life of the party. You might be a high maintenance makeup diva who wishes she could get away with being low maintenance. You could be an outdoorsy gal wishing you could find comfort in a dress and heels. Instead of wishing your life away trying to be someone you were never intended to be; just be you. Don't be afraid to be you, don't be ashamed to be you, and don't try to change you. Here are a few thoughts that may help you:

1. Don't be something your not

You will never be truly happy trying to be something you are not. Don't live your life trying to impress others or fit the mold of someone else. Be you. God made you who you are. Live that life beautifully and contently.

2. Don't compare yourself to others

Comparison is the thief of joy. You will not live a joyful, confident life if you are always comparing yourself to someone else. You will never measure up and you will never find your self worth if you are constantly looking at others. Live your own life and keep your eyes on the Lord. Sure we all have things we would love to change, but don't try to find your self-worth by comparing yourself to others, you will only find yourself lacking and then, be miserable.

3. Find your confidence

A confident lady is the most beautiful kind of a lady. True confidence comes through Jesus Christ and not in your looks. You will never reach perfection in your outward appearance; but you can find peace and contentment with the Lord. You can be happy being you, with wrinkles, bulges, cellulite and all. You can have confidence and learn to love yourself.

So, be you! Everyone else is already taken. Learn who you are, figure out your likes and dislikes and be you. Uncover your own style and personality, and then be true to yourself. Discover your personal convictions and standards and take a firm stand on what you believe. God did not create you to be a chameleon to just blend in the background and hide. He created you to be a light so you could stand out and sparkle and shine for Him. But you can't do that if you are timid, ashamed, or afraid to let that light shine. Be you, and be a confident you!

Chapter Three

Diamond In The Rough

A "Diamond in the Rough", I have heard this statement all my life and most likely, you have too. But have you ever wondered what it actually means? It's basically when someone's good qualities are hidden or when you cannot see the beauty of something, such as a diamond or a jewel, when it is in its rough natural state (not yet cut and filled with brightness). It's hard to ever imagine a diamond as anything other than a beautiful jewel that sparkles. And boy, do we ladies love how diamonds sparkle!

We adore the way they glitter in the sunlight and shimmer when the light catches them just right. There is a reason we refer to them as "bling-bling", because that is just what they do. They bling and it delights us. They are called *"a girl's best friend"*. And whether you are attracted to the flashy exuberant diamonds, or the small simple modest ones, the truth is, we love our diamonds.

But diamonds are not brought into this world with the glitz and the glam that we associate them with. Nope.

The journey of a diamond is an extensive and complex procedure that takes time. Diamonds are formed deep inside the earth throughout many different countries. They are mined, sorted, polished, and cut. This is a very lengthy process. Then, they must be sent to labs to determine the grade of the diamond. And finally, they are sent to jewelry stores around the world to be show-cased for us to drool over.

These steps do not happen quickly, neither do they happen over night. It's a process that takes patience, hard work, and the experience of an expert Master Craftsman. And once this has all happened, the final result is quite priceless.

Isn't this a lovely picture of how we as Christians are? God searches for us in the deepest, darkest, dirtiest places and takes us in our yucky, messy condition. He sees our potential and value. He patiently loves us and begins to take all the unnecessary filth and roughness away. He gracefully chisels away the areas that do not allow us to sparkle and begins to polish us to shine. It's not a fun process and it may take years. But in the Master's skilled and experienced hands, we can become a beautiful diamond that sparkles and shines. However, we must allow Him to chisel and polish, because He will not force any of this process upon us.

We must be willing to humble ourselves into the Master's hand and then trust His plan and purpose. Will it be easy? Will it come without pain or without cost on our part? There may be pain and the process may be long and be very hard. The Bible says in I Peter 5:10b-11, *"...after that ye have suffered a while, make you perfect, stablish, strengthen, settle you, to him be glory and dominion for ever and ever. Amen."* The process to perfection will not be an enjoyable one; but if we humble ourselves to the Master Designer, the process will be worth it. He can take our rough, rugged, messy, filthy lives and transform them into a beautiful, strong, sparkly clean life that shines for Him. He is the Designer and He knows what is needed in our lives and what needs to be taken out. We must trust Him and the process.

Once a diamond has been through the entire process of extraction and refining (the mining, the crushing, the separating, the greasing, the cutting) then and only then will they become valuable. As a Christian, this should be our ultimate goal, to be a valuable life for the cause of Christ. But we can not skip through the process.

All polished diamonds are unique, yet every diamond is valuable. Diamonds come in many sizes, shapes, colors, and various internal characteristics. Even though each diamond is completely different, they each have one common factor; they sparkle and shine. However; they do not have their own light and can not shine in the dark. So what causes a diamond to sparkle and shine or even glow?

A diamond is a conglomerate of many different tiny mirrors all angled in different directions. So a diamond is doing nothing more than reflecting what's in its environment. Hum, does this sound familiar? We are a mirror that reflects our environment as well. We can not shine if we are never around The Light.

Many factors contribute to the value of a diamond such as the color, the cut, the clarity, and the carat weight. As I was reading and studying diamonds; I came across an interesting article on the grading process of diamonds by Knox Jewelers and Lumera Diamonds that I found quite fascinating and perfectly applicable to the Christian life. Diamonds are determined by cut grades and separated into five different classes. Let's take a look at these five grades shared by the experts and see how light affects each on differently.

1. Excellent

For the most precise and beautifully-crafted cuts, light will reflect a subtle angle and radiate throughout the surface of the diamond. Only the most well-cut stones receive this rating. No symmetry defects visible at 10x magnification.

2. Very Good

An impressive rating that many diamonds strive to achieve. The stone will look stunning under multiple lighting conditions and in different environments. Any defects are extremely difficult to see at 10x magnification.

3. Good

A diamond rated "Good" will have a balanced brightness, fire, and scintillation score under varied lighting conditions. Any defects are difficult to see at 10x magnification.

4. Fair

Average diamonds with a passable brightness, fire, and scintillation profile will achieve a "Fair" rating. Defects are noticeable at 10x magnification, and may be visible to the naked eye.

5. Poor

Defects are visible to the naked eye and should be avoided in all cases. For this reason, most jewelry stores do not carry diamonds with a poor grade.

Looking at these five cut grades, I can't help but compare these to the Christian walk. I don't know about you, but I want to be "Excellent". I want to sparkle and shine as brightly as possible and I would love my defects to be hidden as much as possible. Sure, **Very Good, Good, and Fair** are all nice and fine. Yes, they still sparkle and shine, but I want to be more than average. I want to live my life to the fullest and strive to be my best. I will never reach perfection, but excellent sounds pretty good to me. One day I will stand before my Master Designer; my desire is to hear Him say, *"Well done thou good and faithful servant."*

The ideal diamond will capture light from its surroundings and display a beautiful show of color and light that captivates your eyes. It will display a clear spectrum of stunning colors as light strikes its surface, it will sparkle radiantly and emit light. It will be bright and luminous. Just as a diamond reflects light and becomes a priceless treasure that is sought after by hundreds of people; so is a Christian lady who completely radiates the Light of Christ. We are what and who we surround our lives with. Just like a diamond, we are nothing more than a mirror that reflects our surroundings and environment.

Are we surrounding ourselves with The Light? It is the only true way for our light to shine. We must be

reflecting Him. That means we must be spending time with Him and we must be filling ourselves with Him daily. We can not reflect Him if He is not in us. So today, let's spend time with our Father, letting Him rekindle our light by making it stronger and brighter so we can effectively sparkle and shine in a dark and dull world for the glory of God.

Chapter Four

Confident Not Conceited

Have you ever been around a conceited girl? It does not take long before you want to take off and run away from her. No matter how pretty she may be, if she knows it and flaunts it, it is just not very appealing. But on the flip side, have you ever met a beautiful girl and she was so negative, insecure, and down on herself that you felt all the life being sucked out of you when she came around?

I believe that God wants us to be confident, secure, happy women! As women of God, we should not be a self-centered snob neither should we be a Debbie-Downer! There should be a balance. We should be a secure, confident lady that shines her light to a dark world. We should have a confidence that others are drawn to and a self-assurance that attracts the lost world to us. We should not think we are better than others, because quite frankly, we are not. We are sinners saved by the grace of God. So how could we base our confidence in our looks, accomplishments, or in our job title? Our confidence should come from the One to Whom we belong.

Conceited means- *vain, narcissistic, self-centered, arrogant, proud.*
Confident means- *self-assured, positive, assertive, poised.*

There is a big difference in the two words and there should be a big difference in us as Christians. As a Christian, we should have confidence. We should be self-assured, positive, assertive and yes, even poised. Not in a vain, self-centered, arrogant, proud way, but in a humble way. It almost sounds like an oxymoron doesn't it. I'm telling you to be confident, but be humble. So, let me explain.

Confident yet Humble

Be confident because we are a child of God.
Be humble because He gave His only begotten Son and gave His highest treasure for us.

Be confident because we are an heir to the throne.
Be humble because He is the King of Kings.

Be confident because through Him we have forgiveness of sins.
Be humble because He made the ultimate sacrifice to pay for those sins.

He alone is the reason we can have confidence. There is nothing worthy about us. There is no reason for us to feel we have the right to be conceited, vain, arrogant, or proud. The Bible has a lot to say about a proud and haughty spirit. So, before you go around thinking you are "Somebody Special" and strutting around like a "Proud Peacock" maybe you should apply some of these verses to your life.

Proverbs 11:2
"When pride cometh then cometh shame: but with the lowly is wisdom."

Proverbs 16:5
"Every one that is proud in heart is an abomination to the Lord: though hand join in hand, he shall not be unpunished."

Proverbs 16:18-19
"Pride goeth before destruction, and an haughty spirit before a fall. Better it is to be of an humble spirit

with the lowly, than to divide the spoil with the proud."

Proverbs 29:23

"A man's pride shall bring him low: but honor shall uphold the humble in spirit."

Galatians 6:3

"For if a man think himself to be something, when he is nothing, he deceiveth himself."

When you think of a proud arrogant person, what are some of the bad characteristics you think of? I asked myself this question and made a list of what came to mind when I thought of a prideful person. Then I examined my own life and quickly saw that I had many of these negative qualities in me. It was not easy to see such ugliness in myself, but I had to be honest and ask God for His forgiveness if I wanted to have a pure and humble heart.

This would be a wonderful exercise for you to do as well. Make a list or find verses, examine your life and see if there is any pride in your heart that you can ask God to remove.

This is the list that I came up with when I thought of a prideful person and how God worked on my heart in the process.

1. Someone who brags a lot

Proverbs 26:12

"Let another man praise thee, and not thine own mouth, a stranger and not thine own lips."

While in my mind, I think of a proud person as someone who is constantly bragging on themselves; but God says don't brag on yourselves at all. It's not our job to toot our horn or to sing our own praises. God doesn't want us to lift ourselves up; He wants us to lift others up.

When I examined my heart, I quickly realized that I was guilty of bragging. There are times when I have lifted myself up to look good in front of others. There have been many times when I wanted people to know the good deeds I had done, or the wonderful way I handled a certain situation. But the book of Matthew shows me what God thinks of my bragging.

Matthew 6:1-4

"Take heed that ye do not your alms before men, to be seen of them: otherwise ye have no reward of your Father which is in heaven.

Therefore when thou doest thine alms, do not sound a trumpet before thee, as the hypocrites do in the synagogues and in the streets, that they may have glory of men. Verily I say unto you, They have their reward.

But when thou doest alms, let not thy left hand know what thy right hand doeth:

That thine alms may be in secret: and thy Father which seeth in secret himself shall reward thee openly."

God wants to reward me for doing good deeds and He wants to bless me when I help others. But when I brag on the wonderful things I think I have done and the great way I have helped others, then the praise of man and the smiles of others becomes my blessing. Seems foolish doesn't it. Sounds like I'm cheating myself out of a true reward! I don't know about you, but I sure don't want to settle for a temporary moment of praise, when I can have a reward from God that will last a lifetime.

So let's remember, that yes, a prideful person is one who brags on themselves a lot, but we are just as guilty when we feel the need to brag on ourselves, even if it's just a little.

2. Someone who looks down and makes fun of others

Philippians 2:3

"Let nothing be done through strife or vainglory; but in lowliness of mind let each esteem other better than themselves."

Have you ever been with a group of friends when the subject turned onto a poor innocent victim who wasn't there to defend themselves, and before you knew it the gossip was way out of hand? Have you ever been around someone that constantly feels the need to make fun of other people, tearing them down while laughing and joking as if somehow that makes it okay? It's in times like these that you have an opportunity to let your light shine.

So do you?

A) Join in the fun, say things you later regret knowing that you don't really mean what you are saying but, you really want to fit in and be accepted. How can you let your light shine if you are not accepted right?

B.) Yell at all your friends and put them in their place for being rude and stuck-up snobs, then quickly remind them that Jesus would never act like that (WWJD for goodness sake!) and dramatically march off thankful you are not a sinner like them.

C.) Don't say a word, just stand there feeling uncomfortable at the way they are tearing down a close friend.

D.) Is there another option?

While taking classes for my Masters of Education, I had the privilege of sitting under JoJo Moffitt a few semesters. To some of you that name means nothing at all, but to many of you that name automatically brings a smile, maybe even a laugh. This sweet amazing Christian lady has the remarkable gift of living life like no other. She has an incredible way of laughing through the trials of life and lovingly praises God during heartbreaks and disappointments. She has written several books and she speaks at ladies conferences around our country. She brings laughter, smiles, joy, and wisdom to everyone she is around. Her happy nature is infectious and she has a way of making you feel better about yourself when you're around her.

I learned many things in her class. I still remember like it was yesterday when she shared with us just how she handled a situation similar to this, and without her knowing it, she gave us an option D.

So ladies, here is our D:

D.). When others are talking negatively about someone, remember you have a chance to let your light shine. You don't have to speak negative words to fit in and you don't have to yell at anyone and defiantly put them in their place. Instead, kindly and honestly, bring up all the wonderful positive things you can about the person being talked about. If the mood doesn't change and you can tell your positive perspective will not change the negative atmosphere, then try to change the subject. If that still doesn't work, you may need to politely excuse yourself from the group.

For some this many seem foolish or a little over the top. But for those of us who are trying to honor God with a humble heart, this is gold. To live a life where we esteem others above ourselves is living a life that pleases God. We can not tear others down while lifting God up, it just doesn't work like that.

Matthew 12:36
"But I say unto you, that every idle word that men shall speak, they shall give account thereof in the day of judgment."

James 3:10
"Out of the same mouth proceedeth blessing and cursing. My brethren, these things ought not so to be."

The Bible has much to say about our words, and if this is an area you struggle with (we are all human, so I would say we all struggle in this area) then find some verses, memorize them, and ask God to help you learn to esteem others.

3. Someone who makes me feel bad about myself
Ephesians 4:29
"Let no corrupt communication proceed out of your mouth, but that which is good to the use of edifying, that it may minister grace unto the hearers."

It's a rotten feeling when you are talking to someone and they make you feel inferior and insecure. I don't like being around someone who makes me feel bad about myself; like, somehow I just don't measure up to them. In fact, I stay away from people like that. I just don't have time for negativity like that. But evaluating my heart and examining my life, I know I have been guilty of the very crime that I loathe. And because we are all human, I know that at sometime in your life you must have offended someone as well.

We all have room to grow and areas to work on. This might be my biggest goal in life, to edify others and make them feel better about themselves. I desire for others to feel valuable and to know their worth. I want to encourage others and minister grace unto them. But if I am too busy building myself up, I can't build others up.

God tells us to use our communication to edify others. So, let's all try it today. Let's build someone up, encourage and minister good to them. Imagine someone saying, "Wow, she makes me feel so good about myself!" Now that's a goal.

4. Someone who is self-centered
Philippians 2:3-4

"Let nothing be done through strife or vainglory; but in lowliness of mind let each esteem other better than themselves. Look not every man on his own things, but every man also on the things of others."

I naturally think of an arrogant, prideful, conceited person as one who is self-centered. Someone who is always putting their own self first and making the world revolve around them. But God's way of thinking is so different than mine. He tells me not to look to my needs but to others. He tells me to esteem others up over myself. He tells me to put others first and when I don't, I'm self-centered. I may not go around talking about "me, myself, and I"; but when I put myself first, that's what I am doing. When I look honestly into the mirror, I have to admit, that I am a very self-centered person, and I don't like what I see. It's ugly and far from Christ-like but honestly, I like to have my way, I like getting what I want, and I wouldn't mind if the world revolved around me.

I'm not going to lie; this point is a hard for me. I wish I could push a magic button and magically change overnight. But I don't have that button, and I don't have the ability to change myself. Oh, I might improve for a day or two, but I somehow manage going back to my old selfish way. However, I am not hopeless. I have a powerful, loving Father who wants me to come to Him. He knows I am a sinner and He needs me to realize that I need Him. He is forgiving and ready to help me in my weakness. 2 Corinthians 12:9 *".....My grace is sufficient for thee: for my strength is made perfect in weakness. Most gladly therefore will I rather glory in my infirmities, that the power of Christ may rest upon me."* Praise God, I don't have to be perfect! I just rest on the One who can perfect my weakness.

I'm not sure where your weakness lies, whether it is having too much pride in your heart or not having any confidence. I believe that both are a sin. God wants us to be balanced in this area. He wants us to be humble and confident. It's not easy, but with Him it's not impossible. Deuteronomy 31:6 *"Be strong and of good courage, fear not, nor be afraid of them: for the Lord thy God, he it is that doth go with thee; he will not fail thee, nor forsake thee."*

I recently saw a billboard for a plastic surgeon and written in big bold letters was the slogan, *"Confidence brings power"*. I couldn't help but feel sad that so many people have fallen for this false advertisement. The lie that *"If I can just be pretty enough, skinny enough, loved enough, popular enough, if I could only have more IG followers and likes, then I too can have confidence and I can have the power to do anything."* Ladies, confidence does not come through being beautiful, skinny, popular, or even rich. Hollywood's most elite group of the rich and famous has proven this time and time again.

Confidence comes through having a secure relationship with the One who gives confidence. We can have confidence in Jesus Christ and through Him we can let our lives sparkle and shine. Confidence is a beautiful thing and can be used for the glory of God. There is something so rare and so valuable about a lady who humbly holds her head up with confidence while lovingly lives her life for others. Let's build each other up, by complimenting one another and bragging on each other. You never know how your uplifting words may encourage another person.

Imagine a church, a community, a world where women were confident enough to lift up other women. Be that radiant light that builds someone else up in encouragement and prayer instead of tearing someone down and destroying them. This is the type of lady I desire to be. My prayer is that perhaps you will desire to be a confident lady shining bright, inspiring and helping others.

Chapter Five

A Royal Princess

We have all watched the movies, read the books, dreamed the dream, wished for it, played it, and imagined it.

I'm talking about a Fairy Tale Princess.

As little girls, it was our biggest fantasy. We wanted to hear every story, own every dress-up gown, and watch every movie about a Princess. There is just something about a Princess and her beautiful gowns that captivate us all. We are all suckers, from the smallest pig-tailed little girl, to the most mature seasoned lady.

Maybe it's because a Princess is unique, different, rare, gracious, beautiful, and kind. Maybe it's because she lives a life we can only dream about, in her beautiful gowns and sparkling jewels, in a huge castle with servants. Maybe it's because she is the daughter of a King with royalty streaming in her blood.

Then there is another type of Princess that is even more fascinating. You know the story; it's the one about an ordinary girl who meets a handsome Prince riding on a white horse. They fall madly in love, get married, and live happily ever after. Oh, there is just something about a girl who gets a Prince! It's magical when an ordinary girl becomes a Princess.

I think that is why most of the world has fallen completely in love with Kate Middleton. I would dare say that almost the entire universe watched her wedding. All eyes were glued to the television. Every woman anticipated to see what her dress would look like, what type of veil she would be wearing, how her hair would be styled, and what color flowers she would carry. Why? Because, she is a modern day fairy tale! She was just a normal girl who became a Princess. If you are like me, you love to see how she dresses everyday and you love to hear her speak. We adore the pictures of her beautiful family. She has such grace and humility, yet she is confident and poised. We just can't seem to get enough of her.

I believe this is how Christian ladies should be. We should be wrapped in grace and humility, yet have the confidence of a princess. There should be something different about us. We should walk different and talk different. We should have all the confidence that Kate Middleton has. We have the ability to be self-assured, positive, and poised. Not because of **Who** we are, but because of **Whose** we are.

We belong to the King of Kings, and we are a Princess.

We are a child of the King.

Yes, we belong to the Royal family.

We are a Princess!

We are that ordinary girl that the King of Kings took into His Royal Family.

We are also a modern day fairy tale.

However, I believe we should live in a manner that is a little different than the Royal Family. There should be some differences in our lives.

1. We should be approachable

I don't know about you, but I don't think I would throw myself on top of the Queen and give her a big ole hug. There are rules and protocols you have to follow when you are in her presence. In the olden days, if you came before the King uninvited, he could simply order, *"off with your head"* if it pleased him. But the King of Kings has a different way of ruling His kingdom.

In Hebrews 4:16 He says, *"Let us therefore come boldly unto the throne of grace that we may obtain mercy and find grace to help in the time of need."* We have an amazing God who is totally approachable. We do not have to fear coming before Him because He wants us to come to Him. He even said we could come boldly before Him. As Christian ladies, we should live in the same mindset. We should be approachable to the people around us. We should never give others the impression we are better than them. We should not be stand-offish. We need to be the type of ladies people know they can run to in the time of need.

2. We should draw people to us

The Royal Family attracts attention everywhere they go. People are drawn to them. They want to be near them, see them, and hear what they have to say. Our King was also this way, but He drew people in a different way. He served the people. He ministered to the people and preformed miracles for them. When word got out about this Miracle Healing Man and what He could do, people flocked to Him. Men, women, boys, and girls wanted to see Him. They wanted to be near Him. They wanted to hear what He had to say. I believe this is how we should live. We should live in such a way that it draws others to us.

James 4:8 says, *"Draw nigh to God, and He will draw nigh to you..."* We should have such a walk with God that people can feel His presence on us. Others should want to be around us because they know there is something different about us. We should draw people to us, not because of who we are, but because of Whose we are.

3. We should live our lives differently

Because all eyes are on the Royal Family, they have to live life in a different manner. There are some places they can not go and some things they just can not do. And I believe as a child of the King, we are representing the King of Kings in everything we do. There are some places we should not go and some things we should not do. There are words we should not say, drinks we should not drink, music we should not listen to, clothes we should not wear, friends we should not have, and jobs we should not take because it does not bring honor to our King. As an heir to the throne, we must live our lives differently knowing that people are watching us. We do not want to be a stumbling block for the ones who are watching us.

Now wait a minute, you are going just a little too far with all of this Royalty stuff!!!

Am I? 1 Corinthians 10:31 has a little to say about this. *"Whether therefore ye eat, or drink or whatever you do, do all to the glory of God."* Everything we do as a Christian reflects back to God. It will either bring honor or dishonor to His name. I Corinthians 6:19-20 goes on to say *"What? Know ye not that your body is the temple of the Holy Ghost which is in you, which ye have of God, and ye are not your own? For ye are bought with a price: therefore glorify God in your body, and in your spirit, which are God's."* Although this is not popular teaching in today's society, we live in a *"if it makes you happy, then do it"* generation. But that is a very ungodly way to live. We are to do what makes God happy and He calls us to be different, holy, and live in a manner that pleases and glorifies Him.

This is why so many people do not want to go to church or have anything to do with God. They see how many Christians live Monday- Saturday. They see there is no difference between them. So why should a lost person want Jesus? Why should they go to church? Why should they sacrifice a day off? That is a great question.

I pray my life and your life will be lived in such a way it naturally draws people closer to God. Let's shine a light that shines so bright that the lost world wants what we have. May we have a kindness so rare and so genuine that everyone around us knows there is something different about us. We need to live a holy life. A life that reflects God and makes the lost world want and crave what we have.

*We should be different.
*We should have peace the world can not understand.
*We should have joy unspeakable.
*We should extend mercy and grace to others.
*We should be hard workers and honest.
*We will not be perfect, but we should try to never be a stumbling block.
*We should be approachable.
*We should live like royalty.

There should be places we don't go and things we do not do. Not because we are better than anyone else, but because we represent the King of Kings and we should desire to bring Him glory through our lives.

What better way to sparkle than to be a Princess!

Chapter Six

Don't Get It Backwards

Have you ever been out in public and discovered a particular piece of clothing was put on inside out....ugh! It's a terrible feeling when someone walks up to you and points it out. No matter how polite they are, you can't help but feel foolish. You wonder how in the world you could have gotten it backwards. How could you have been so careless? How did you not notice? Worse yet, when your tag is hanging out, waving to everybody and it's a size you don't particularly want the world to take note of. Yes, it is frustrating and embarrassing, but the bottom line is, you got it backwards. The inside is made for the inside and the outside is made for the outside. When put on wrong, it's backwards.

Have you ever grabbed a cup out of your cabinet and just before you poured your drink into it, you noticed the inside of the cup was not clean? Oh, the outside looked clean and spotless, but the inside was yucky. You know, with that crusty kind of filth that the dishwasher somehow glued on there. No matter how clean the outside is; if the inside is dirty, you can bet your bottom dollar, ain't nobody drinking out of that. The outside can sparkle, but if the inside is filthy, it does no good.

I think a lot of times, we as Christians seem to get it all backwards. We seem to focus so hard on the outside, trying to perfect our "Christian Image" that we totally neglect the inside. We may try everything in our power to make the outside sparkle, but if the inside is filthy, we have it backwards. Oh, we may fool those around us for a time, but eventually the outside will shine through. Just like a tag hanging out of a shirt that's been put on backwards, waving for all to see. The filthy inside will eventually spill out for everyone to see.

The Bible says in Matthew 23: 26-28

"Thou blind Pharisee, cleanse first that which is within the cup and platter, that the outside of them may be clean also. Woe unto you, scribes and Pharisees, hypocrites! For ye are like unto whited sepulchers, which indeed appear beautiful outward, but are within full of dead men's bones, and of all uncleanness, Even so ye also outwardly appear righteous unto men, but within ye are full of hypocrisy and iniquity."

For years, I was guilty of this. I tried so hard to be the perfect Christian. I had this image of what I thought this should look like and I put all of my energy into achieving this goal. I focused hard on pleasing people, saying the right things, volunteering for everything, and trying to look perfect on the outside, but I had it all backwards. While I was trying to look righteous on the outside, I was not being righteous on the inside. God wants us to focus on our insides. He wants us to clean the inside up first, then take care of the outside.

So how should we focus on our insides? How do we go about cleaning all the dirty rotten things out? Didn't we become clean and spotless when we were saved? Yes, we became a new spotless creature the day we were saved, but we still have to live in our sinful flesh and in a sin cursed world. Because of this, it doesn't take long for that spotless creature to get the filth and the grime of sin all over it again. This is why it is utterly important to have a daily walk with God. Even though it can be discouraging to know we have to fight daily against our sinful nature, we are not without hope. The Bible is full of promises, hope, and guidelines on how we can live a victorious Christian life and how we can work on having a clean heart and a righteous life.

Galatians 5:19-23

*"Now the works of the flesh are manifest, which are these; Adultery, fornication, uncleanness, lasciviousness (lust), Idolatry, witchcraft, hatred, variance (strife), emulations (rivalry), wrath, strife, seditions (troublemaking), heresies, envyings, murders, drunkenness, revellings (being wild), and such like...**But the fruit of the Spirit is love, joy, peace, longsuffering, gentleness, goodness, faith, meekness, temperance...**"*

It can become a bit overwhelming and seem almost impossible to measure up to this list of things to clean out. But instead of cleaning out all the bad things, let's just focus on putting all the good things in. The good list will automatically take care of the bad list. It's challenging, but with the help of the Lord, it is not impossible.

Notice these wonderful attributes are called the *Fruit of the Spirit.* I believe if we walk in the Spirit, we will see His fruit in our lives. That's why it is so important to have a daily walk with God and daily yield to the Spirit. I believe this is why Paul said we need to "die daily". It's a daily fight between the flesh and the spirit, but the one we feed the most, is the one who will come out winning.

So, how do we feed our Spirit? We must simply give our spirit its spiritual food, the Bible. If you go weekly, monthly, or even yearly without ever reading your Bible, then you are spiritually starving. There is no way you can fight the flesh on your own. To clean up the inside, you must have a daily walk with God. To truly sparkle and shine for God, your life must reflect Him and His characteristics. And in order for that to happen, you must spend time with Him. Just remember, the real you, always shines through. You can't fake a relationship with God.

Don't get it backwards ladies; don't let your main focus be on the outside, take care of the inside first.

In I Samuel 16, Samuel was looking for a man who would be the future king of Israel. While he was looking for a man who would fit the description of what he thought would make a good king, God had a different idea. Look at verse 7, *"But the Lord said unto Samuel, Look not on his countenance, or on the height of his stature; because I have refused him: for the Lord seeth not as man seeth; for man looketh on the outward appearance, but the Lord looketh on the heart."* And we see in this chapter that God did not choose the big, strong men, he chose a shepherd boy to be the future king of Israel.

Ladies, let's sparkle and shine for God. Not with a perfectly polished outward appearance, but with an inward glow that's so strong it radiates onto our outward appearance. Remember, this can only come with a relationship with our Heavenly Father! Spend time with Him today, and don't get it all backwards!

Chapter Seven

A Valuable Lady

I am a lady. I am a wife, a mother, and a homemaker. I am feminine. I am a girly-girl, and a tad bit high-maintenance (okay, a lot high-maintenance). But being a feminine, high-maintenance, stay-at-home mother does not make me a worthless doormat or a second-class citizen. My value does not come from my precious husband, my lovely child, the amount of money I make (or don't make), my accomplishments, the denomination of religion I am, who I voted for, or the size dress I wear. My value comes from the King of Kings and the Lord of Lords. My worth comes from the One who loved me so deeply, He sent His Son to die for me. This is where my value lies. I am loved and I am cherished.

I am a little tired of this lie that the world has created, that to be a valuable woman, you have to be career driven, have a big house, a new car, and hundreds of followers on social media.

The world paints a picture of the new modern woman

as one bad, tough, rough woman with a perfectly toned body, a very successful job, a big house, and someone who doesn't have cellulite...ugh! This woman can do it all and doesn't take anything from anybody. She is a woman with a hard heart and a strong backbone. She is someone who doesn't show her feelings, share her heart, or open up to anyone. She knows how to get the job done without help and doesn't need a man. She depends only on herself. She lives only for herself, her dreams, and her career. She is more concerned about how much money she can make, than the people around her. She might consider herself a powerful independent woman, and if she is extreme, she proudly calls herself a nasty woman. This woman does not need anybody, and certainly not God.

To be honest, I don't like this picture that the world has painted of the new modern woman. Here are a few reasons why:

*I am not a heartless creature; I am loved by the Creator.

*I am not a robot; I am a woman full of emotions.

*I am not Superwoman; I am a woman who needs others.

*I am not a hard-hearted woman; I am a lady with a tender heart.

*I can not find my value in social media; I find my value in the Son of God.

*I can not find my worth in a successful career; I find my worth in my relationship with my Savior.

*I am a cherished, loved, valuable, sensitive, worthy woman, who wants to live my life for others, showing them the love of God.

Is there anything wrong with being a strong, independent, hard working woman? Nope, not at all! In fact the Bible has much to say about women, their character, and their work ethics. Let's take a look at the most popular lady in the Bible, the Virtuous Woman from Proverbs 31. She was one tough cookie who knew how to work hard, provide for her family, and tend to their well being. But the difference between this "Virtuous Woman" and the "Modern Woman" is that the Proverbs 31 lady had a tough backbone wrapped in wisdom, grace, virtue, honor, gentleness, and kindness.

Proverbs 31:10-31

"Who can find a virtuous woman? For her price is far above rubies.

The heart of her husband doth safely trust in her, so that he shall have no need of spoil.

She will do him good and not evil all the days of her life.

She seeketh wool, and flax, and worketh willingly with her hands.

She is like the merchants' ships; she bringeth her food from afar.

She riseth also while it is yet night, and giveth meat to her household, and a portion to her maidens.

She considereth a field, and buyeth it: with the fruit of her hands she planteth a vineyard.

She girdeth her loins with strength, and strengtheneth her arms.

She perceiveth that her merchandise is good: her candle goeth not out by night.

She layeth her hands to the spindle, and her hands hold the distaff.

She stretcheth out her hand to the poor; yea, she reacheth forth her hands to the needy.

She is not afraid of the snow for her household: for all her household are clothed with scarlet.

She maketh herself coverings of tapestry; her clothing is silk and purple.

Her husband is known in the gates, when he sitteth among the elders of the land.

She maketh fine linen, and selleth it; and delivereth girdles unto the merchant.

Strength and honour are her clothing; and she shall rejoice in time to come.

She openeth her mouth with wisdom; and in her tongue is the law of kindness.

She looketh well to the ways of her household, and eateth not the bread of idleness.

Her children arise up, and call her blessed; her husband also, and he praiseth her.

Many daughters have done virtuously, but thou excellest them all.

Favour is deceitful, and beauty is vain: but a woman that feareth the LORD, she shall be praised.

Give her of the fruit of her hands; and let her own works praise her in the gates."

She is one tough momma, but one godly lady.

What an amazing difference between the "Virtuous Woman" and the "Modern Woman"!

*The virtuous woman has a servant's heart and wraps her toughness with gentleness and kindness.

*She lives her life for others.

*She fears the Lord.

*She allows her husband to be the head of the home.

*She is an extremely hard worker.

*She put her family first.

*She takes care of her employees and those within her household.

*She is a homemaker, yet works hard outside the home.

As a lady of God,

*I want to be: independent but 100% dependent on God.

*I want to be strong but gentle.

*I want to have backbone but be gracious.

*I want to be firm but be compassionate.

*I want to be tender-hearted but not a push-over.

*I want to be humble but know my value.

*I want to stand firm on my beliefs but show immeasurable kindness.

*I want to a hard worker but not hard-hearted.

*I want to have balance and keep my priorities in check.

*I want to live my life loved by the Creator of the Universe.

*I want to be a lady that sparkles and shines for Jesus and not a woman that reflects the ways of the world.

I am a valuable treasure, one that was paid for at a great price and I don't want to ever forget that. Maybe you have lost sight of your true value. Maybe you are trying to find your value or you are seeking for it in all the wrong places. Please know that no amount of success, money, muscles, designer shoes, or purses will ever give you the permanent worth you are seeking for. Oh, you may find temporary glory, fame, and contentment, but just like snow on a warm sunny day, it will soon melt away. Only our value and worth in God will last a life time.

I Corinthians 6:20

"For ye are bought with a price: therefore glorify God in your body, and in your spirit, which are God's."

God paid the ultimate sacrifice for you. You are very valuable to Him. So live as a virtuous lady who knows her self-worth and knows her value. You do not have to make your own way in this hard, stressful world as a rough, tough woman. No, you can live life as a soft, gentle, kind, gracious lady who knows how to stand firm on what she believes. You can glorify God in your actions and in your character as you live victoriously for Him. You can sparkle and shine for the Lord knowing you are His and you are a very valuable treasure.

Chapter Eight

The Best Kept Beauty Secret

It is no secret that women desire to look their best. We want flawless skin and a glowing complexion. We want to feel young and keep the wrinkles away. We all desire to keep our youth and secretly wish there truly was a Fountain of Youth somewhere on this planet. But unfortunately, age has a way of sneaking up on all of us. Age is no respecter of persons, and it leaves its marks for everyone to see. Some women are willing to pay any amount of money for the latest product that promises youth and glowing skin. And others of us just wish we could afford it! Right?

Unfortunately, there is no product, surgery, or pill that can keep the wrinkles away. Yes, you can stretch out those wrinkles with surgery and hide them for a time. You may prolong the process, but eventually, it will catch up with you, find you, and leave its evidence behind. Aging, as dreaded as it may be, is a natural process of life, and you simply can't stop it. But don't be disheartened, there is a beauty secret that has stood the test of time. It's a beauty secret that guarantees a super-natural, beautiful, glorious, amazing glow. A glow in fact so fabulous, it will grab the attention of others. It doesn't matter what your age is, how many wrinkles you have, or how deep the bags under your eyes are. This beauty tip will offer success. It's the best kept beauty secret, and I am going to share it with you today!! Are you ready? You may want to get some paper and a pen because this will change your entire beauty regimen. There is only one way to get that natural, beautiful, sought-after glow.

A WALK WITH GOD

Yep, that's it! There is no magic solution, lotion, or pill. There is no substitution for this process and there are no short cuts. You can not buy it. You can not borrow it from someone else. It is very plain and simple. You must walk with God. You may ask how does a walk with God and a relationship with Him give you natural beauty and a glowing countenance?

Let's look in Exodus 34. In this chapter, Moses has been spending time with God on Mt. Sinai writing the Ten Commandments. When he comes down from the mountain the children of Israel noticed that Moses' face is shining. Exodus 34:35 *"And the children of Israel saw the face of Moses, that the skin of Moses' face shone..."*

His face was shining because he had been in the presence of God Almighty. He had been with the Light and his countenance reflected that Light. Ladies, we can not reflect a light that does not exist. If we do not spend time with God, then we will not have His Light. We can put the most expensive makeup on our faces and use all the night cream there is on the market, but that will never take the place of a relationship with Him. You can not fake it. You either have a light or you do not. This glow comes only through a relationship spent with Jesus. You either have it or you do not. Psalms 4: 6b "...*Lord, lift thou up the light of thy countenance upon us.*" May this be our heart's desire!

The words below are from a popular praise and worship song. Study the words and make it a prayer.

Shine Jesus Shine

Lord, the Light of Your Love is shining,
In the midst of the darkness shining
Jesus, Light of the World, shine upon us
Set us free by the truth You now bring us,
Shine on me. Shine on me.
Shine Jesus shine,

Fill this land with the Father's glory
Blaze Spirit blaze,
Set our hearts on fire.
Flow river flow,
Flood the nations with grace and mercy
Send forth Your Word,
Lord and let there be light.

Lord, I come to Your awesome presence,
From the shadows into Your radiance,
By the blood I may enter Your brightness,
Search me, try me, consume all my darkness.
Shine on me. Shine on me.

As we gaze on Your kingly brightness
So our faces display Your likeness
Ever changing from glory to glory
Mirrored here may our lives tell Your story
Shine on me. Shine on me.

I love the line, *"As we gaze on Your kingly brightness, so our faces display your likeness."* This is my desire, to mirror the image of God and display His likeness, and I think this should be the goal of every Christian lady. We should reflect God in all we do. If our faces display the likeness of God, what would that look like?

*Holiness
*Godliness
*Righteousness
*Gentleness
*Kindness
*Tenderness
*Thoughtfulness
*Peacefulness
*Meekness

If we reflected these beautiful characteristics, we would definitely have a glow that would light up a dark room. But you can not wave a flameless candle in a dark room and expect to shine light. Neither can you sparkle and shine if you do not have the Light. So many times we women totally miss it. We get so busy focusing on all the outer details that we miss the main beauty step, our hearts and our relationship with God.

I love fashion, I love makeup, and I obsess over jewelry, purses, and shoes. I enjoy getting all dolled up and looking my best. But this can not be my focal point or my main focus in life. If I am depending on clothes, accessories, make-up, and big hair to find my self-worth; then I have missed the mark.

I Peter 3:3-4 *"Whose adorning let it not be that outward adorning of plaiting the hair, and of wearing of gold, or of putting on of apparel; but let it be the hidden man of the heart, in that which is not corruptible, even the ornament of a meek and quiet spirit, which is in the sight of God a great price."*

I Timothy 2:8-9 *"In like manner also, that women adorn themselves in modest apparel, with shamefacedness and sobriety; not with broided hair, or gold, or pearls, or costly array; but (which becometh women professing godliness) with good works."*

I am guilty of falling into the trap of thinking "Oh, if I only had that outfit, I would be so happy and content. It will make me feel good about myself" or "Man, if I could just get that purse, I will be accepted by my co-workers." or "That expensive lipstick will make me prettier." Yes, we all want to feel pretty and beautiful. We want nice clothes, pretty hair, and radiant skin and there is nothing wrong with that. But maybe we should rely more on God for our beauty and less on materialism and makeup.

Psalms 90: 17a *"Let the beauty of the Lord our God be upon us..."*

Just imagine the beauty of the Lord upon you. Friend, we must change our way of thinking. The Bible encourages us to put the emphasis on our hearts and focus on being godly, not on our outer appearance. Does this mean that enjoying fashion and make-up is a sin? No, not at all! But when we are consumed by it and it becomes our number one priority in life, we have become distracted. Ladies, let's not get side-tracked on outer beauty. Don't let reality TV and Hollywood influence you into being consumed with your looks. We live in a day where the emphasis is on a woman's beauty instead of her heart.

I Samuel 16:7 *"...for the Lord seeth not as man seeth; for man looketh on the outward appearance, but the Lord looketh on the heart."*

Our hearts have a way of telling off on us. You can try to fake a relationship with God, but before long the real you will shine through. What does your heart say?

Does your heart say:
   *You are vain?
   *You have your priorities wrong?
   *You have gotten distracted?
   *You need a renewing?

*You need time with God?

*Your relationship with God is questionable?

Or does your heart say:

*You have walked with God?

*You have an unshakeable relationship with God?

*You have an undeniable, unexplainable glow about you?

*Your priorities are in order?

*You are renewed, refreshed, and recharged?

What does your heart say?

Remember the saying; *your eyes are the window to your soul?* Well, if you want that glow on your face and that sparkle in your eyes, then remember, it's not something you can put on. That sparkle and shine comes from what you put in. It's the time you spend with God. It's the relationship that you have built with Him in Bible reading and in a prayer life. It's being in the presence of the Light and allowing His source of Light to flow into your soul. It's His Light shining in your soul that illuminates your eyes and brings a beautiful glow onto your face. There is no substitution for it. There is no short cut for it. There is no age limit. It is available for all.

Money can't buy it and the world can't claim it. It is the best kept beauty secret, and it's available for you and for me. It's the only way we can truly sparkle and shine in a dark and dreary world.

Chapter Nine

Do My Reactions Reflect God

Our very first home was a foreclosure and it was in pretty bad shape. We bought it because we could see the potential that this house had. My husband, being a do-it-all kind of guy, knew he could transform this run-down house into a cozy, loving home. So, we began the journey of a fixer upper. He took one room at a time and slowly began to remodel the house. It was such an exciting time. I distinctly remember how eager I was to start painting, decorating, and adding all those special touches to create that homey environment that we longed for. When it was finally time to start the decorating process of our four bedroom two bath fixer upper, I became a little overwhelmed. Like most newlyweds, we didn't have much furniture at all. So, I relied heavily on thrift stores, clearance aisles, and even the side of the road! Yep, I am that girl.

I remember being a little stumped with the main bathroom. It had an old 1970's medicine cabinet for a mirror. Its broken edges and outdated style was just horrible. I knew without a doubt it had to go. So, I started my hunt for mirrors and quickly found out that the size and style mirror I wanted was way out of my budget. I was a little bummed with that dose of reality, but you can't get a girl on a mission down for long. I quickly decided to try out Goodwill. I vividly remember the day I found my bathroom mirror. It was like finding a needle in a haystack. It was a true treasure. It was in need of a little TLC but the potential was all there. It was a fun and simple project. I painted the mirror and gave it a distressed look. I loved the character on the frame of the mirror and the end result was absolutely fabulous. It was definitely the piece that brought the bathroom out of the 70's and added the final touches to create a fresh, clean, modern bathroom.

That mirror also reminded me of a great truth. Just like a mirror will reflect an image, my reactions also reflect an image. And I have to wonder, do my reactions reflect God? For years I have heard the saying *"You can not control the actions of others but you can control your reactions."* While I believe this to be true, I do not always live like I believe it. It is usually after I raise my voice, cross my arms across my chest, clench my teeth, roll my eyes, stomp down the hall, and slam the door that the shame and guilt sets in and I think, *"Well I could have handled that differently."* My reaction did not reflect God at all. Nope, I failed that opportunity. That was more along the behavior of my 4 year old son when he is told NO! Whether we react in a temper tantrum or the silent treatment, are we honoring God in our reactions?

Surely God understands that I am human and I get angry! Sometimes I just blow up. It's just who I am and besides, He made me. It's not like it's my fault that my button gets pushed one to many times and then I snap.

Ever had this argument with yourself or with God? Ever tried to justify your behavior? Yes, God gave us emotions. He understands we get angry, but He also commands that we *"be angry and sin not."* While this may seem absolutely impossible, God never gives us a command that He does not follow up with instructions and hope. James 4:8 says, *"Draw nigh unto God and He will draw nigh unto you."* The closer we draw to Him, the closer He will draw us to Him. I love this hope and promise. The closer we get to Him, the more like Him we will become.

The more time we spend in His Word, the more we will resemble Him. Galatians 5:22-23 shares some of His wonderful characteristics that He wants us to have. It is a list of the Fruit of the Spirit. Love, joy, peace, long-suffering, goodness, gentleness, meekness, faith, and temperance (which is self- control) Yep, there it is. Ouch! God wants and expects His children to resemble Him and have self-control. In 1 Corinthians 13:7, we are challenged to have charity and to bear all things and endure all things. The powerful words of Psalms 119:165 says, *"Great peace have they which love thy law: and NOTHING shall offend them."* Those are some mighty bold words. However, they are not mine, they are God's. He said if you are getting offended and your feelings are getting hurt; instead of pointing the finger at the other person, look in the mirror and realize you do not love His law. Wow! How convicting is that? We all know that if you do not love something, it is because you do not spend any time with it, you are not invested in it, or you do not pray for it. That is what God is saying. You are not spending time with Him and you are not invested in Him. You most likely have your eyes on the situation or the problem, and not on Him.

Maybe you have different reactions due to an entirely different situation. Sickness may have you defeated; loneliness might have you drowning in depression. The loss of a loved one may have you struggling for a purpose to live. Not being able to bear children may have you consumed with bitterness. Extreme insecurities may have you chained up in bondage.

No matter what you are going through dear friend, we all have hope. While all of our struggles may be different, all of our reactions can be the same. How?

We must choose to let our reactions reflect God.

May we choose to bring Him glory in all of our actions and reactions. It may not always be easy or convenient, but may we choose to honor Him in this area. Do my reactions reflect God or do my reactions reflect the lack of time I have spent with God? What does your reflection say? I challenge you to look in the mirror, take a deep look and ask yourself, **"Do my reactions reflect God?"**

II Corinthians 3:18
"But we all, with open face beholding as in a glass the glory of the Lord, are changed into the same image from glory to glory, even as by the Spirit of the Lord."

Chapter Ten

A Renewed Right Spirit

Not too long ago, I had to totally walk away from writing. I took a break from blogging, writing, working on this book, and I also took a big step back from social media. I realized that I was going through a dry spell and found that I had no words. I had nothing to share and nothing to give. I was empty. Kind of like a water fountain that's out of water and is all dried up.

Have you ever been there?

For a few months I felt like I needed a break. I felt a desperate need for a recharge, refocus, and a renewed spirit. In short, I needed a heart transplant. I did some evaluating and what I noticed was not pretty. In fact, it was down right ugly. While I was reflecting and trying to put this season of emptiness into words, this little poem came into my head. To my amazement, the words just started flowing out and I knew this had to be from God, because I am, by no means a poet. So please, forgive my feeble attempt!

A Heart Transplant

When I took a good look at me
I saw things I did not want to see.
I noticed I was becoming someone
I did not want to be.
I was often way too snappy
and seldom joyful or happy.
I felt way too stressed and moody
but desprately wanted to be chill and groovy.
I did not want to feel angry or mad
I wanted to feel peaceful and glad.
I wanted to laugh and feel care-free
But even that seemed so impossible for me.
And no matter how hard I tried to be more
A self-made change was just not in store.

Not knowing what else to do,
I turned my eyes upward to You.
I put my pitiful heart in your hands
And trusted that You had better plans.
You are truly the only One
that could get this heart transplant done.
With tears in my eyes I gave you my heart
Knowing my fears would soon depart.

Peace filled my heart as I looked from the skies,
No longer would I believe the devil's lies.

Praise God!
He heard my heart's cry
In His strength and His mercy, I can rely.
Never alone,
are we left here to roam.
He is with us all of the way
Every step of every day.
When we leave our troubles in the Master's hand
He will give us the strength that we need to stand.
~Dorothy Gates~

Yes, I needed a heart transplant and I needed it bad. I was in a dark funk. I was stressed, frustrated, moody, grumpy, troubled and often down-right angry. And the worst part of it was I didn't even know why! I knew I needed a change; something real, and something permanent. Sure, I had mastered the *"fake it till you make it"* approach. And I knew how to plant that fake smile on my face and appear as if all was right with the world. But deep down, I was not okay, I was miserable, and I was causing those around me to be miserable. Now, let me clarify that while I was going through this confusing, frustrating time, I NEVER doubted my salvation, my relationship with God, or His goodness. I knew I was simply going through a funk or a fog, if you will. It was a thick fog and it was doing its best to rob me of my joy. However, I knew there was a Light at the end of the tunnel. I trusted that Light and ran for it. In my darkness and in my state of fog that Light seemed to shine brighter and stronger and I clung to it hoping for a brighter day. But in order for that change to happen, I had to be honest with myself. I also had to remember that I was not alone or forsaken. God was right there with me in that fog. He was shining His light and waiting patiently for me to run to Him.

I would like to share some of the steps I took during this time. I know everyone's journey is different but this is what helped me and if it can help you then I know my time in the "fog" was not in vain.

1. Cling to God

Even when you don't feel like it, you must stay close to God. Cling to Him as if your life depends on it. I continued to read my Bible, pray, attend church, and I clung to God. There were days I did not want to, or feel like it; but I did. I knew I needed God and I knew I had to be faithful to Him. I knew during this time, I needed more of God, not less of Him. The best thing I found for me to do was to continue my normal daily routine, even when I did not want to. I also tried to take a step back from things that were being a distraction (for me it was TV and social media) and focus on all the good positive things in my life. I listened to devotions by amazing ladies of God, I read powerful books from godly ladies, and I listened to good gospel music. Even though you may not feel like this is helping; feeding your spirit is benefiting you in ways you can not see.

2. Cling to His promises

Even in those darkest days, His promises had healing powers and renewed a hope in me. Even when I did not feel Him working on me, He was! Even in the most hopeless situation, cling to His precious promises. I held on to promises from the Bible. I wrote several verses down and would refer to them several times throughout the day. Here is a great verse that offered so much comfort during this time: II Corinthians 4: 8-9 *"We are troubled on every side, yet not distressed; we are perplexed, but not in despair; persecuted, but not forsaken; cast down, but not destroyed."*
Psalms is loaded with wonderful promises of God and is a great book to read during hard times.

3. Be honest and get to the root of the problem

I am normally a very positive, happy, sincere person. I enjoy life and want to live it to the fullest. My deepest desire is to live an amazing life for God. So, when I noticed I was being grumpy, moody, unkind, negative, and sometimes just down-right angry, I knew I needed to get to the root of the problem. At first, I tried to hide it, cover it up, and pretend that nothing was wrong. Oh, it worked for a few hours, and maybe even a few days. But eventually, that suffocating, joy-robbing funk seemed to come back. It was when I decided to be honest, dig deep, and go to God for help that healing actually began to occur. I also learned it was okay to NOT be okay. God does not expect perfection, but he does desire honesty. Healing did not happen immediately or overnight. It was a process, it took time and determination. It was not easy; but praise God, I can say healing came!

4. Memorize Scripture that applies to your need

I knew I needed a heart renewal. So, I searched the Bible for verses that applied to that topic and began to memorize them. I quickly noticed that my brain doesn't retain information like it did when I was younger. So I put verses on sticky notes, and hung them on my mirror. I also wrote some of them down in my prayer journal, put some on the fridge, and anywhere I knew I would look throughout the day. I knew I needed to repeat these verses several times a day to get them to stick in my brain. Repetition is the key to learning for me. The Bible says, *"If ye abide in me and my Words abide in you, ye shall ask what you will and it shall be done unto you."* John 15:7

Here are a few of the verses that truly made a difference during my fog and I will explain how God led me to these verses and how they applied to my life. I knew I needed a renewed, restored, recharged, right spirit, so I started with **Psalm 51:10** *".....renew a right spirit within me."* This was my go-to verse; it was the very first verse that came to my mind and the one I quoted over and over and over. I knew I didn't have the right spirit and I needed the right one. My mind couldn't help but ask God, *what is the right spirit?* Quickly, the next verse came to mind, **Galatians 5:22-23** *"But the fruit of the Spirit is love, joy, peace, longsuffering, gentleness, goodness, faith, meekness, temperance..."* I knew I desperately needed these qualities in my life, and this verse needed to be stamped in my mind and pressed deep into my heart. After reflecting on this verse, I noticed that the very first fruit of the Spirit is love (I don't think that was by accident) God then led me to this next verse and I knew He was showing me I needed love, love, and more love.

I Corinthians 13:4-8 *"Charity (love) suffereth long, and is kind; charity envieth not; charity vaunteth not itself, is not puffed up, Doth not behave itself unseemly, seeketh not her own, is not easily provoked, thinketh no evil; Rejoiceth not in iniquity, but rejoiceth in the truth; Beareth all things, believeth all things, hopeth all things, endureth all things. Charity (love) never faileth"*

Wow! Kinda seems that Love is the answer to every problem. Oh, but wait...God is love, so yeah, it kinda is the answer!!!

Other verses that helped were:

Proverbs 17:22 *"A merry heart doeth good like a medicine but a broken spirit drieth the bones."* I knew my spirit was broken, but God's promise of joy was like a spoonful of medicine to my weary heart.

II Corinthians 4:16 *".....the inward man is renewed day by day."* This verse served as an important reminder that to have a permanent right spirit, I had to be renewed every day.

And then I clung to Psalm 23:3a *"He restoreth my soul..."*

5. Claim those promises and put your trust in God into practice

I remember the day the missing step hit me like a ton of bricks. It was as if I had been putting a puzzle together and was at the very end when I realized the last piece was missing. You see, I was reading my Bible, praying, memorizing wonderful scriptures, but I had been doing all the work. I was trying to make the change. I was trying to be a happy person, a better mother, a lovable wife, but I was failing and I was failing miserably.

Why? Because I was trying to make the change!

The day the answer hit me, I was pouring my heart out to God. I was talking, crying, begging, pleading, sulking, and whining when it hit me (right in the heart). The powerful verse from Psalms 46:10 *"Be still and know that I am God."* It was as if God was saying, "Shh...Be quite! Be still and listen to me. I've got this, rely on me and let me be God."

Let Him be God?

Yes, the answer was plain and simple.

Let God be God.

He is the God of Abraham, David, and Paul.

He is the God of the universe, and He is my Father.

I have a great big wonderful God. Nothing is too hard or impossible for Him. He alone had that power to change my troubled soul, and He was the missing puzzle piece.

I'm not sure why I had made Him so small and I'm not sure why I tried to do all the work. But that day, I apologized to God. I had not relied on God to fix the problem. Yes, I had prayed and told Him I had a problem, but I had not trusted that He would solve the problem. That was the day my burden was completely lifted off my shoulders and the healing was truly complete. Peace immediately flooded my soul, and joy quickly took the place of the stress and anguish that I had been holding on to. What a special day that was for me, when I let God be God and gave Him the burden I was trying to fix. 1 Peter 5:7 *"Casting all your cares upon Him for He careth for you."*

6. Put your pride aside

Probably the hardest lesson for me to learn during this time, was putting my pride aside and realizing I didn't have it all together. Soon after I made things right with my Heavenly Father, I had to seek forgiveness from my sweet family. Saying "I am sorry" is not easy for me. I'm not sure why, they are just three little words, but my-oh-my are they awfully hard, powerful words. I can not even express the joy that came with those three humbling words; but once I said them, I felt an over abundance of joy. You may wonder why I needed to apologize to my husband and my sweet little boy. Well, who do you think took the blunt of that moody, grouchy, frustrated, stressed out, and sometimes down-right angry person? Yep, the two most important people in my life! I was ashamed and I knew I had to put my pride aside and make things right with them.

(Side note: I'm thankful that God gave me a husband who puts up with my bad days and loves me when I am not loveable. It has made me love him all the more!!)

Now, I am not saying I have not had a bad day since this time, but I did get recharged, renewed, and basically had a heart transplant. I knew I needed a change and I desired to allow God to *"create a right spirit in me."* I do not know why we have to go through hard times or fogs in our life, but I do know if we allow God to have the glory, it will not be in vain.

Honestly, I struggled with sharing this season of life with you. I guess I like to act like I have it all together, I imagine most women do. And I don't like to admit I have shortcomings. (AMEN??) But, I truly desire to be relatable and honest. I recently came across a verse and the truth had such an impact on me, I cried like a big old baby. I knew then that God wanted me to share my heart and my struggle. II Corinthians 1:3-4 *"Blessed be God, even the Father of our Lord Jesus Christ, the Father of mercies, and the God of all comfort; Who comforteth us in all our tribulation, that we may be able to comfort them which are in any trouble, by the comfort wherewith we ourselves are comforted of God."*

If we never have troubles, struggles, or dark days, God would never be able to comfort us. If we have never been comforted by God, how can we truly comfort others? If we comfort others with the love of God, we are using our sufferings for His glory, and maybe just maybe, we can show the world the love, mercy, kindness, and goodness of our Heavenly Father. And then perhaps we can truly sparkle and shine for Him.

Chapter Eleven

The Power of the Tongue

In this social media driven generation, people have been given the misconception that they have the right to speak their mind. There is this false idea that they can be brutally honest, say whatever they want, and have no sorrow, remorse, or consequences for their behavior. Slandering, bullying, and hating are now socially acceptable. In fact, the idea of holding your thoughts, opinions, and words back would now mean you are not being *true to yourself*. As long as it is what you believe to be true and how you feel; then it is A-Okay.

Is it any wonder that depression, therapy, and suicide are at an all time high? Is it a coincidence that the pressure of drugs, alcohol, skin cutting, and immorality is affecting even young children?

Ladies, in order for our lights to sparkle and shine for the Lord, we must use our words for the glory of God. We must choose to be an encourager and not a discourager. To be effective for the Kingdom, we have to decide to build others up and not break them down. Our words should draw people to us and ultimately point them to Christ.

The Bible has much to say about our words, our mouth, and our speech. In fact a great portion of Proverbs is dedicated to comparing a wise man to a foolish man. Many of these verses deal with comparing how they use their mouth and how they handle situations. So, for the sake of application let's say a wise woman and a foolish woman, and let's look at the vast difference in their speech and in their actions.

A Wise Woman Will Use:

1. Wise Words

One of the distinct differences between a wise woman and a foolish woman is the way she handles herself, her mouth, and her words. A wise woman chooses to use wise words. She uses discernment, good judgment, and understanding when she speaks. Let that sink in for just a moment. She discerns the situation, uses good judgment, and tries to understand the outcome of her words before she speaks. In other words, she thinks before she speaks. She may even ask herself, will my words:

1. Help or hurt the situation?
2. Offer encouragement or discouragement?
3. Bring happiness or heaviness?
4. Radiate a solid relationship with God, or reflect a backslidden heat?
5. Show wisdom or foolishness?

"The mouth of the righteous speaketh wisdom and his tongue talketh of judgment." Psalms 37:30

"The mouth of the just bringeth forth wisdom..." Proverbs 10: 31a

"She openeth her mouth with wisdom; and in her tongue is the law of kindness." Proverbs 31:26

2. Edifying and Encouraging Words

A wise woman will use every opportunity she has to edify and encourage others. She uses her mouth to build others up; not break them down. As a wise woman, she sees the need to uplift her sisters in Christ. We are working together, not against each other, and we are not in competition with one another. We are on the same team and we should be rallying around each other. But unfortunately, it is not this way in most churches. Women are often backbiting, gossiping, complaining, and tearing each other down. A wise woman's speech should offer grace, not grief.

"Let no corrupt communication proceed out of your mouth, but that which is good to the use of edifying, that it may minister grace unto the hearers."
Ephesians 4:29

3. Gracious Words

A wise woman will chose to use gracious, merciful, pleasant, courteous words; not harsh, cruel words.

"The words of a wise man's mouth are gracious...."
Ecclesiastes 10:12

4. Thoughtful and Thought-out Words

A wise woman will think before she speaks. She uses well-thought-out words and does not use word vomit! It is hard to control our mouth in the heat of the moment, but a wise woman will choose to use wisdom; even when steam is blowing out of her nostrils. She counts to ten, thinks of the right words to say before she just spews them out. Oh boy! This is a hard one. I wished I could say that I didn't ever struggle with this, but thank the good Lord in Heaven, He is willing to help even the toughest of cases like myself. There is help for the helpless! But we must beg God for wisdom and obey when He pricks at our heart to bite our tongue. And let me tell you, I have literally had to bite my tongue to keep it shut! So much so, I thought I was going to bite it completely in half. We must be walking with God and in wisdom so we can be prepared for these situations.

"Let your speech be always with grace, seasoned with salt, that ye may know how ye ought to answer every man." Colossians 4:6

"Wherefore, my beloved brethren, let every man be swift to hear, slow to speak, slow to wrath." James 1:19

"The heart of the righteous studieth to answer..." Proverbs 15:28

5. Soft Words.

A wise woman does not yell, scream, or raise her voice when things are not going her way. She doesn't have to be gruff, crude, or hurtful to get her point across. Instead she knows how to softly use her words and gently, lovingly, firmly, and wisely handles even the toughest conversations and situations.

"A soft answer turneth away wrath..." Proverbs 15:1

6. Wholesome Words

Wholesome means good, moral, clean, virtuous, pure, innocent, proper, decent, harmless, and squeaky clean. Does this describe what flows out of your mouth? A wise woman decides to use wholesome words and there is no room for gossip, lies, cursing, backbiting, or drama.

"A wholesome tongue is a tree of life." Proverbs 15:4

7. Acceptable Words

A wise woman knows that her words need to be acceptable and pleasing to God! And just imagine, if our words are pleasing and acceptable unto Him, how much more will they be accepted by the people who need them.

"Let the words of my mouth and the meditation of my heart be acceptable unto you, O Lord." Psalms 19:14

"And whatsoever ye do in word or deed, do all in the name of the Lord Jesus..." Colossians 3:17

"The lips of the righteous know what is acceptable..." Proverbs 10:32a

8. Spirit-filled Words

A wise woman knows that there will be times the words that come from her mouth can not be her own words, but must be Spirit-filled words. A wise woman will allow God to lead her to the right words in order to impact the lives of others. There are crucial times when a wise woman will get out of the way and let God direct her.

"Then the Lord put forth his hand, and touched my mouth. And the Lord said unto me, Behold, I have put my words in thy mouth." Jeremiah 1:9

9. Guarded Words

A wise woman will guard her mouth and use caution, reservation, and restraint when choosing her words.

"Set a watch, O Lord, before my mouth; keep the door of my lips." Psalms 141:3

10. Healing Words

A wise woman's words are like a healing balm to those around her, adding comfort, cheer, and reassurance.

"Pleasant words are as an honeycomb, sweet to the soul and health to the bones." Proverbs 16:24

11. Hushed Words

A wise woman knows when to keep her mouth shut. Sometimes the best thing we can do is to say nothing at all. It's not always the easiest but sometimes it's the best.

"In the multitude of words there wanteth not sin: but he that refraineth his lips is wise." Proverbs 10:19

"Whoso keepeth his mouth and his tongue keepeth his soul from troubles." Proverbs 21:23

"He that hath knowledge spareth his words: and a man of understanding is of an excellent spirit.
Even a fool when he holdeth his peace, is counted wise: and he that shutteth his lips is esteemed a man of understanding." Proverbs 17:27-28

If you want to see where you are spiritually, then put James 1:26 to the test. *"If any man among you seem to be religious, and bridleth not his tongue, but deceiveth his own heart, this man's religion is vain."* A wise woman knows that sometimes it's just best to say nothing at all.

Now, let's look at a foolish woman and the vast difference in the way she chooses her words.

Foolish Woman Will Use:

1. Foolish Words

A foolish woman's mouth is just the opposite of a wise woman's. Her speech is full of thoughtless, rash, reckless, ill-considered, impolite, unintelligent words. She lacks good sense, judgment, and wisdom. So obviously, her speech will be filled with foolishness.

"...but the lips of a fool will swallow up himself. The beginning of the words of his mouth is foolishness: and the end of his talk is mischievous madness."
Ecclesiastes 10:13b-14

"...but the mouth of fools poureth out foolishness."
Proverbs 15:2b

2. Hasty Words

A foolish woman will quickly give you a piece of her mind at the drop of a hat. She never thinks or prays about what she should say, or how she should handle a situation. She is like a walking volcano waiting to spew out hot lava.

"Seest thou a man that is hasty in his word? There is more hope of a fool than of him." Proverbs 29:20

"A fool uttereth all his mind: but a wise man keepeth it in till afterwards." Proverbs 29:11

3. Angry Words

Angry words tend to add more fuel to the fire. Just like a flame immersed with gasoline has a tendency to explode, if it's not managed it gets out of control very quickly. Angry words also make things worse and never defuse a situation. A foolish woman does not know how to handle her reactions, her temper, or her words. She does not fight fair, and typically spits out hostile words that are very unnecessary. She quickly loses control of her mouth, her temper, and the entire situation.

"A wrathful man stirreth up strife..."
Proverbs 15:18a

"...but grievous words stir up anger."
Proverbs 15:1b

"...but violence covereth the mouth of the wicked."
Proverbs 10: 11b

"Be not hasty in thy spirit to be angry: for anger resteth in the bosom of fools."
Ecclesiastes 7:9

4. Evil Words

The definition of evil is wicked, bad, wrong, foul, sinful, dishonorable, corrupt, and vicious. When you are spreading gossip, lies, drama, or half-truths, you are choosing to use evil words. A wicked woman has no regard as to how her evil words may destroy or hurt the lives of others. Ask yourself if you are choosing righteousness or wickedness when you are talking about your friends and family. Don't allow evil words to sneak into your conversations.

"...but the mouth of the wicked poureth out evil things." Proverbs 15:28b

5. Dishonest Words

You can not believe or put much value in what a fool has to say. The book of Proverbs mentions a forward heart and a forward mouth several times. Frowardness in modern terms means to be willfully contrary to someone, to be crooked, twisted, distorted, backsliden, or basically someone you can not put your faith and trust in. Doesn't this seem to define a dishonest man perfectly?

"Put away from thee a forward mouth, and perverse lips put far from thee." Proverbs 4:24

"...but the mouth of the wicked speaketh forwardness." Proverbs 10:32b

"...and he that uttereth a slander, is a fool.1" Proverbs 10:18b

6. Meaningless Words

I saved this point for last because we all have fallen guilty of this at some time or another. We have all used words that have no purpose, meaning, or use. We just talk to talk, or talk to be heard. That could be why most women have been known as having the "the gift to gab". We, as women do not need help talking. We naturally enjoy talking and fellowshipping. There is nothing wrong, foolish, or sinful about this. (Thank goodness!) But it is in those fun times of fellowship that we must remember to guard our mouth and have wisdom. It is so easy to get caught up in conversations that becomes meaningless and can easily lead to gossip. Gossip never leads to edification, but only leads to destruction. You may try to justify your gossip as just catching up, or sharing a prayer request amongst your closest friends. You may not see the harm in meaningless words, and honestly, neither did I until I came across this verse; and it shook me to the core.

"But I say unto you, that every idle word that men shall speak, they shall give account thereof in the day of judgment. For by thy words thou shalt be justified, and by thy words thou shalt be condemned."
Matthew 12:36-37

Ladies, our meaningless, idle words will one day be judged by the Ultimate Judge. There is destiny in words. Read, study, or memorize Matthew 12:33-37. Let's beg God to help us with our words. Let's not be a foolish woman that has no control, care, or thought about the things that spew out of our mouth. Let's be wise, kind, and thoughtful with the words that proceed from our lips.

As Christian ladies, we must let our lights shine into a dark world. We must show our neighbors, community, family, and friends that there is something rare, special, and unique about us. Our lights will not shine if we are using our mouth foolishly. Proverbs 31:26 says it beautifully, *"She openeth her mouth with wisdom; and in her tongue is the law of kindness."* What a challenge this verse is. The Proverbs 31 Woman, known as a woman more valuable than rubies, gives us a guideline for our mouth. Open it with wisdom and use our tongue for kindness.

"Out of the same mouth proceedeth blessing and cursing. My brethren, these things ought not so to be." James 3:10

*Are our words a blessing or a cursing?
*Are our words helpful or hurtful?
*Are our words wise or foolish?
*Are our words healing or destructive?
*Are our words encouraging or discouraging?
*Are our words life or death?

"Death and life are in the power of the tongue..." Proverbs 18:21

*There is power in our words.
*There is destiny in our words.
*There are consequences to our words.
*The choice is ours!

Will we be foolish or will we be wise with our words? While the rest of the world is bashing, slandering, and giving everyone a piece of their mind, we as Christian ladies can be a light. We can radiate, we can encourage, and we can uplift others for the Kingdom of God. We can use our words wisely and sparkle and shine in a dark and dreary world.

Chapter Twelve

Changing our "Why God?" into "Wow God!"

Have you ever asked the question, "Why God, why me?" If you are a human and your heart is beating, then there's a pretty good chance you have. No matter how great of a Christian you are, how much faith you have, or how much you read the Bible; there will be times in your life when certain situations bring you to your knees asking God, "Why??"

For the most part, I pretty much live my life with unwavering faith in God. I have a very optimistic personality and see the good in situations. (Most of the time) However, there have been heartbreaks, disappointments, and struggles that have left me wondering "Why?" Some of those situations, I can now look back on and say, "Oh, I get it now, thank you God!" And then there have been times that have left me utterly amazed saying, "Wow God! You are so good, thank you, thank you, thank you!" Such is the time when

God struck my heart with the thought of how He alone can change our "Why God?" into "Wow God!" You see, God took me on a journey and during this journey I was filled with doubt (lots of doubt), a little bit of bitterness, and even some resentment. But God's sweet love and mercy took me out of the dark dungeon of doubt and set me on the beautiful mountain of mercy.

It all started on a beautiful snowy, icy day which ended terribly, leaving my husband and me in the ER. This dreadful evening comes into my mind very clearly, every detail still raw and fresh as if it were just yesterday. It was the night my husband and I were in a terrible car wreck and the night I was first told I would never have children. The story begins when we were on our way home from work. Due to an unexpected snow and ice storm, it didn't take long for the roads to become dangerous. There was not much of a warning, and many people were forced to drive home from work and school in these hazardous conditions. Because of my lack of experience driving on snow and ice, we decided to meet up at my husband's office, leave my car in town, and ride home together in his truck. We actually juggled the decision of which vehicle to take, but my husband wisely decided at the last minute to drive his truck instead of my car, in case we had any issues. A rather small decision that we later learned saved our lives. We drove very slowly and carefully down the slippery roads and were only five miles from home, when I mentioned to my husband that I trusted his driving, but I did not trust the driving of the other drivers on the road. Honestly every time we passed oncoming traffic, I got nervous and closed my eyes and held my breath. It seemed the words were no longer out of my mouth when my husband shouted "Hold on!" I looked up just in time to see a large SUV heading straight towards us. The driver had obviously hit ice and lost control of his vehicle.

I closed my eyes and grabbed on to the handle of the door, as if bracing for the impact. It took only seconds for the two vehicles to collide into each other and for the horrific crash to be over. But in those few seconds it literally felt like an eternity. I remember the unexplainable feeling of everything happening in slow motion. Life had instantly been jerked out of our control. I remember the terrible sounds of metal hitting metal, the sickening sound of glass shattering into a million pieces, the blunt force of my body being slammed back and forth several times into the dash board, and the truck being slammed once again into a ditch.

I recall how it felt as if a pause button had suddenly been pushed and almost immediately everything came to an immediate stop. Then came the worst part, the bone chilling, eerie sound of complete silence! For what seemed like an eternity was in reality just a few seconds but I was terrified to open my eyes to the unknown. In that split second, I was scared that when I opened my eyes I would find myself in Heaven. I quickly tried to take a breath and realized that I had held my breath the entire time of the accident. It was in that breath that I felt a terrible sharp pain in my chest and knew I was alive. Then I was hit with the horrible fear of opening my eyes and turning my head to look at my husband. What if he was not okay? I could not find the strength to open my eyes. I was literally scared to death, and frozen with fear. If you have ever been in a wreck you know the fear I am speaking of. It is an unexplainable fear. The fear of the unknown. The fear of the unexpected. The fear that life as you know it will never be the same.

With my eyes still shut, I began begging God to let my husband be okay, it was then that I heard my husband's frantic voice asking if I was okay. My eyes quickly opened and I looked over at him. I could tell he was okay, but the current situation was not okay. It did not take long to observe that he was trapped in the truck.

It was then that we were somehow snapped out of our slow motion time warp and brought into a rather fast paced state of being. It is in these moments that God showed His love toward us, even though it was unknown to us at the moment. Immediately, people came to our rescue. I could hear them trying to open the jammed doors and offering words of comfort and encouragement. Instructions and commands were being given all around us. Amazingly, one of the volunteer helpers was an off-duty police officer (or an angel) who had already called the accident in and had an ambulance and other officers on the way. We were quickly told by the rescuers that we were a miracle; we should not have survived that crash.

Honestly, the events that occurred after this are all a blur, I was put on a stretcher and put in the ambulance and out of the corner of my eye I saw my husband being rolled in next to me. I do not even know how they got him out of the truck. While the paramedics were getting us situated in the ambulance, a person stopped to help and searched the truck for our cell phones, insurance information, my purse, and my husband's wallet, and his keys. He thoughtfully did this for us, we were in such shock that we never even thought to get these items out of the truck. We were then rushed to the hospital and once there, immediately taken separate ways. We would not see each other again for several hours.

They took me in for several X-rays because my chest hurt terribly and I thought my foot might be broken. After several rounds of MRI, CAT scans and X-rays, they brought me back to a room to wait on the doctor. It seemed like a lifetime had passed before he or anyone else ever came back into the room. The kind, gentle doctor (total sarcasm here) had absolutely no bedside manners or compassion, and didn't seem to have any enjoyment in his job. He bluntly told me that my foot was not broken. Then he quite dryly told me that during the CAT scan they discovered that I had several large tumors in my uterus. He said they needed to be removed immediately. He asked me if I had any children. I was still a little stunned after hearing the word TUMOR that I couldn't find words to answer. So I nodded my head no and wondered to myself if this meant I had cancer or if I was dying. He very abruptly told me that I would never be able to have children and that I needed to have a hysterectomy as soon as possible.

I felt as if he had just kicked me in the gut and slapped me in the face all at the same time. I couldn't breathe and my foot, that I just knew was broken, was sending a sharp pain all the way to my heart; or was my heart breaking from the news the doctor had just given me? I was trying to concentrate on what the doctor was saying, but he was talking so fast and matter-of-factly.

My foot hurt so badly and my brain felt like mush. The next thing I knew I heard him say, "Now don't ask me any questions, save those for your OBGYN." and he literally turned around and left just as quickly as he had entered.

There I was, left alone, confused, and shocked from the terrible pain of the wreck, my heart aching from the terrible news, and I had no one to talk to. The tears began to pour down my face as the words, **"You will not be able to have any children"** rang in my ears over and over and over. I began to pray but my mind began to spin out of control. "Why God? Why me?" It didn't seem fair. I couldn't understand how this could be happening to me. This was not part of my plan or part of my dreams.

This is not fair!

I want to be a mother!

Who is this man to tell me I can't be one?

How would my husband take this news, we had only been married a few short years?

Where was my husband and when would I get to see him?

How was he?

Gracious, was he okay?

Why am I not good enough to be a mom?

I have spent years investing in everyone else's

children! For years I served as a children's church worker, a school teacher, picking kids up for church on a bus or in my car.

I directed children's choir and was the babysitting queen.

Why am I fit to invest in other children, but unfit to have my own?

It's not RIGHT, I'm a good person!

I thought you loved me God...

I could tell I was literally about to lose it. There I was left alone with my crazy thoughts and this heartbreaking news. My body was still in shock and my foot hurt so badly. No one came in to check on me or offer me any medication, and on top of it all, I had to go to the bathroom in the most desperate way. Several hours later, my husband was released and brought into my room. I was a total mess by that point! I was crying uncontrollably. I'm sure my poor husband thought I was dying. I explained to him what the doctor had said. He was very supportive and encouraging. The poor guy had a broken arm and a broken foot, but was far more concerned about me than his own pain and injuries. We were finally released sometime around 2:00 am to go home and start our recovery process. But since we lived 30 minutes out of town and had no transportation home, a police officer drove us to a nearby hotel. Again God showed his love and mercy to us that night when the young hotel clerk happened to be a young college girl I had gotten close to. She quickly checked us in and helped us to our room. She even walked to a near by gas station and bought us some pain relievers, some snack food, and drinks since neither of us had eaten since lunch. This little angel did all of this on her own without being asked. Both of our cell phones died at the hospital and neither of us had our chargers. Of course, no one knows phone numbers anymore but by some amazing coincidence my husband was able to make a call on his dead cell phone to his aunt. She immediately dropped everything drove over an hour to come pick us up. She took us to her house where she nursed us for several days. Again, this was God showing his love and favor to us. Had we gone home, we would not have been able to take care of each other. Neither one of us could hardly walk; we were pretty much out of commission for 48 hours. She was such a precious saint, cooking for us, making sure we had our medications on time, and taking us to our doctor visits. Once we got home we were blessed again by my dad coming and staying with us for a couple of weeks. I don't know what we would have done without our Aunt Wendy and my dad.

Due to our injuries, we both ended up off work for quite a while. I was in physical therapy for my foot, which was not healing. After a month of very painful therapy and new x-rays, the doctor discovered my foot was indeed broken (ha!). My husband's truck was totaled and we were down to one car. Between the injuries, the heartbreaking news of no babies and the never-ending pile of doctor bills, I began to slip into a depression. I would regularly ask God, "Why? Why us?" I just did not understand why all this was happening. With the challenges of trying to heal from the wreck, my visit to the OBGYN was put on the backburner for several months. So I was able to hold on to the hope that she would straighten this whole mess out. She would tell me the ER doctor didn't know what he was talking about.

Finally the day came when I felt physically and mentally ready to make the appointment. The hope that she would correct the silly ER doctor's information was the only thing that had kept me going. However, the day of my appointment, she sadly confirmed what I did not want to hear. I had several large fibroid tumors and due to the location of where they were, it would be impossible for me to have children. She also did not recommend having them removed but also recommended having a full hysterectomy when I was ready. My husband was there with me and could see the disappointment all over my face. We left her office heartbroken, hopeless, and completely helpless. Even in this devastation, we knew we had to trust God. We decided we would put the matter completely in God's hand and we made a hard promise to each other that we would not become bitter. That is not an easy promise when your heart is breaking, and you can not see the light at the end of the tunnel, and your mind is filled with "WHYS".

If you know me, read my blog, or follow me on social media then you already know this is not the end of my story. Nope, it was just the beginning.

But first, let's go back to another big "Wow God!" moment. The man who hit us, did not have insurance and there was some confusion with our insurance. Because of this, we did not think our insurance would cover us or help us with anything. And let me tell you, there is so much more involved in a wreck than you can possibly think about. Yes, you expect the doctor bills and the medicines, but you never think about the towing prices of the totaled truck, the cost of the truck sitting in a junk yard, the $20,000 ambulance ride to the hospital. The therapy, the casts, the boots, the crutches, the X-rays, and

I'm sure I'm missing something, it seemed to be never-ending. I mean the bills were mounting sky high, and we had been out of work during recovery, and on top of it all my husband still needed a truck. I remember collecting all the bills and laying them next to my Bible. I began crying and begging God to do a miracle. I specifically recall challenging God to take care of every penny we were out, and to take care of the money we still owed. I remember reminding Him (like He needed reminding or something...lol) that He owned the cattle on a thousand hills and He could financially take this burden off of us. I don't remember the exact timeline but it was a very short time after that prayer that we received a phone call from our insurance company. They asked us to meet with them and bring in all of our bills. In that meeting we soon discovered that they had corrected their mistake and would indeed take care of every single penny we were out. They wrote my husband a check for his truck, paid the towing company, the junk yard, and they paid every penny to the hospital, the doctors, all of our medicines, and the physical therapy bill. They literally took care of every single penny we were out. And then they even wrote us a check for pain and suffering. I remember looking at that check with tears forming in my eyes and saying "Wow God!"

God answered our prayers and showed us that He is faithful and He will always take care of our needs. I can not tell you what this did for us spiritually and mentally. I am not sure if there is anything sweeter in this life than to personally see a huge miracle happen in your life and to see a prayer request answered. We were reminded in that moment that God indeed loved us and always keeps His promises. What an amazing God moment.

Now for my second big "Wow God!" moment, which is my greatest miracle to date. For the most part, my husband and I were truly happy in our marriage, but I would be lying if I said I never question God, or that my heart did not long to be a mommy. I still asked God "Why". But God does not have to explain why. He works in ways we can never understand. His ways are not our ways, neither are His thoughts our thoughts. What we must remember is that God loves us and He loves to work with the impossible. He loves to heal our broken hearts and He loves to show His power.

In 2013 we had the shock of our lives when we found out we were pregnant. My doctor said it was simply a miracle and she could not explain how it could possibly have happened. But she didn't have to; we both knew it was God. We had put the matter into His hands and He alone would get all the glory from this pregnancy. When my son was born his doctor and the entire nursing staff named him the Miracle Baby, and he truly was. I was allowed to see a modern day miracle preformed in my life. God changed my "Why God?" into "Wow God!" Because of His greatness, I have been able to share my testimony several times and I am able to give Him all the glory. And I try to take care of every opportunity to praise Him, every time someone mentions how cute he is, I am able to share the fact that he is my miracle baby.

Maybe you are going through something too big for you. Perhaps your world had been rocked and your feet have been knocked out from under you. You might feel as if you can not breathe another breath. Maybe your "Why God?" is your health or a financial struggle. Maybe your sorrow is causing a depression you can not get out of. Is it loneliness or rejection, heartbreak, disappointment, or an unattainable desire that has you doubting God? No matter if it is your job, your family, or your church that has left you pleading "Why God?" just remember, He is in control and NOTHING is too big for Him. Give Him the opportunity to change your "Why God?" into "Wow God!" Whatever it is, put it in the Master's hands and let Him take control. Isn't it wonderful that nothing is too big for God? He may not change the situation, but He can give you the strength to get through the situation. He might do a work that is completely different from what you expected, but let Him be God. Let Him have control of the situation. Then trust in Him for the results and the outcome.

The words of the child's song are very inspiring words for us to remember, **"My God is so great, so strong and so mighty. There's nothing my God can not do."** Let your light shine with the knowledge that God is not in Heaven scratching His head wondering how our life got so out of control. He is not bewildered, confused, or shocked. No, instead in II Timothy 1:7 He reminds us, *"For God hath not given us the spirit of fear, but of power and of love and of a sound mind."* And then in Isaiah 55:8 He says, *"For my thoughts are not your thoughts neither are your ways my ways, for as the heavens are higher than the earth, so are my ways higher than your ways, and my thoughts than your thoughts."* God's ways can not always be explained, reasoned away, or justified, but His ways can be trusted, depended on, and rested in. Even though we do not understand, we can be confident that our hope and our faith is in His hands. So what is it today that you need to put in His hands? What is it that has you asking "Why God?" Put it in His control and allow Him to change it into a "Wow God!"

Chapter Thirteen

Don't Let Your Past Mistakes
Dull Your Sparkle

Don't let your past hinder you from shining your light brightly for God. It's so easy to get caught up in the lies that the Old Sly One likes to whisper in your ears. He is an expert at accusing Christians of being unworthy and undeserving. He eagerly waits for opportunities to take past mistakes and smear them all in your face. He loves to tell you that you're unfit and don't have the right to be used by God. He patiently waits for those deadly accusations to defeat you and ultimately destroy you. You know what he says is true. You don't deserve to be used by God. You are unworthy. You want to serve God, but you're scared you will only bring shame and reproach to His name. I mean, what if people found out what you had done, or who you used to be? It's so tempting to believe your past mistakes can determine who you can be, and what you can do for Christ! But thank God, you don't have to allow the "old you" to stop the "new you" from serving God!

The day I published and released my first book **P.I.N.K.** I was immediately hit with self-doubt and insecurities. The old Deceiver did not waste any time hitting me with every negative thought that he knew would successfully smack me right between the eyes. He began to whisper in my ears, *"You are not an author, who do you think you are to write a book? No one will buy it. Your friends will think you are foolish and you will be a complete failure. You will be a disappointment and embarrassment to your entire family. You are a fake and a fraud. Who are you to encourage others? You have bad days and you still sin. You argue with your husband and you snap at your child. Who do you think you are? You are not worthy. You are not qualified. You have too many mistakes in your past to be of any use to God. You have hurt people, how can you think you could help others? You will disgrace your church and be a complete joke to all the people who know you."*

Gracious, he knew exactly what to say and how to hit me hard. I began to question God and His purpose in asking me to write a book. I am not a qualified author. I did not go to college to be a writer. I went to college to be an elementary teacher. I do not have eloquent speech and I often struggle to finds the right words to say. I am very simple-minded, and do not have deep, intellectual thoughts. In fact, I don't even know how to spell intellectual. (Thank goodness for spell check!) I have made so many mistakes. I have failed others, disappointed friends, frustrated my family, argued with my husband, and snapped at my child. Surely God, you didn't really call me to be an author!

While these tortuous thoughts were wreaking havoc in my brain, I suddenly remembered Paul from the New Testament. I thought about all the terrible things he had done and how he had a horrible past. God used Him in spite of his wicked deeds and called him to do all kinds of wonderful things for Him. I was washing dishes when his life and his amazing ministry popped into my brain. I stared out the window for a moment and allowed his transformation to soak into my heart. I threw my rag down into the water and ran to my desk to get my Bible, and began to read in Acts and ponder the grace of God. Paul did not allow his past crimes to hinder him from obeying God. He served God with passion and zeal. He preached the gospel near and far. The same man who persecuted Christians, inflicted pain to the churches, and even consented to Stephen's stoning is the same man who is responsible for writing much of the New

Testament. You mean a murderer, church destroyer, and Christian persecutor could be transformed by the power of God to become one of the greatest authors in the greatest Book ever written? Wow! Talk about the grace and the power of God.

We all have a calling and we all have a purpose in life. It is not our job to reason with God or remind Him of what we are capable of or not capable of. It is our job to trust and obey. We may feel we are inadequate, unqualified, and unworthy. But God sees potential, He sees grace, and He sees the blood of the Lamb. In this beautiful song by Natalie Grant we see the grace of God and how He truly sees us. Let me share part of these touching words with you!

"Clean"
(Natalie Grant)
I see shattered. You see whole.
I see broken. But you see beautiful.
And You're helping me to believe
You're restoring me piece by piece
There's nothing too dirty
That You can't make worthy
You wash me in mercy
I am clean

Thank God, I am clean and even though I am unworthy, I can be used of God. Not because of what I have done or what I can do, but because of what He has done and what He can do! Don't let anything stop you from moving forward for God. Here are a few thoughts to inspire you to keep growing, keep moving, and keep serving God, no matter what your past may look like.

1. Don't let your past stop you

Don't let anything you have done in the past stop you from being everything you can be today. You are not the same person. Just like Saul was transformed to Paul. You too have been transformed. The old man is dead and the new man is now alive. Bury that old man and let him go, move forward with the power of God and allow the new man to live!

"Therefore if any man be in Christ, he is a new creature: old things are passed away; behold, all things are become new." II Corinthians 5:17

No doubt, there will be obstacles to hurdle and mountains to cross, but praise God; you do not have to do it alone. The same God Who sparked a fire in Paul, is the same God Who saved you. He can use you to do great and wonderful things for Him. God has graciously forgiven you of your sins. He has removed your past sins from your life, now you must choose to move forward and claim that victory.

"As far as the east is from the west, so far hath he removed our transgressions from us." Psalms 103:12

2. Don't let Satan's lies influence you

Satan does not want you to succeed. He does not want your influence to reach others and encourage them. He wants you to fail and stay in your past sins. He knows what you can do through the power of God. So he will hit you with every weapon he has. He will lie to you. He will slap you with negative thoughts and insecure words. He will bring your past up and hit you smack dab between the eyes. He is the Accuser and he will faithfully accuse you of every past and present failure. But, the choice is yours. Will you allow Satan's lies to influence you from moving forward? Will you allow your insecurities to destroy your potential?

3. Don't let Naysayers hinder you

I can't help but think of all the Christians that were affected by the persecutions of Saul. My mind wonders about the lives that were wounded and families that were hurt due to his cruel actions. I also wonder how these Christians accepted him after he was saved. Did they welcome him with open arms? Did Stephen's family offer him forgiveness? I would imagine this would have been a very humbling experience for Paul. I can't even imagine the amount of faith it would take to minister to the people he had sought to destroy.

In Acts 9, we see that soon after Paul preached his first sermon there were indeed some naysayers. There were even some disciples who were afraid of him. They did not believe his change was real. There were probably Christians who did not accept him into their fellowship. I can imagine there were several bitter, hurt, resentful Christians who would not offer him forgiveness. There were no doubt churches that did not open their doors for him to preach in and pastors who did not want to work beside him in the ministry. I'm sure it took years for Paul to build trust with his fellow believers. I can assume it was not an easy journey, and more than likely he often felt lonely and guilty with the sins of his past. But the amazing fact here is, no one stopped Paul. He served the Lord and obeyed him. He did not let people's opinions, doubts, fears, negativity, rejections, or skepticism influence his obedience to serve God. He lived for the One who had miraculously changed him, and did not worry about the naysayers.

4. Don't let the journey discourage you

Paul did not become a super Christian over night. In fact, when we see his transformation in Acts 9, we see he sat in total blindness for three days. Then there was a process of healing, eating, strengthening, learning, and growing. God sent a disciple named Ananias to minister to Paul. I don't know how long Paul was in Damascus with Ananias and the other disciples but it's important to notice that this process was accounted for in Acts 9:17-19. During this time, we see he was restored his sight, baptized, and filled with the Holy Ghost. Don't neglect the importance of this journey. There must be a time of healing, restoring, and a time for spiritual growing. These steps must not be skipped, but don't get down-hearted or discouraged. Look in the very next verse, verse 20, *"And straightway he preached..."* Once he began his ministry, he did not waste any time. He didn't let insecurities slow him down. He jumped to it.

Don't skip the important steps and don't let your spiritual journey discourage you. You may have ups and downs. You might have bumps along the way. But don't give up. Keep moving, keep growing, and keep serving God. The journey may take longer than you want it to, but trust God for His perfect timing.

So Ladies, don't let your past stop you from serving God and don't let Satan discourage you from doing miraculous things for the Lord. Don't be afraid to let your light shine bright for the entire world to see. Let that light overpower your past and all your shame. Live victoriously for Him and in His power. Don't be ashamed to sparkle and shine for the One who has given you the light. You just never know how God can use your story and your testimony to reach others. Don't let anyone or anything hinder you from obeying God.

Chapter Fourteen

Building a Dream House

What is your idea of a Dream Home? An old white country farmhouse nestled safely beside a massive, aged oak tree with a weathered wooden swing hanging from one of its sturdy branches?

Maybe a wooden cabin on the lake with a big screened-in back porch that offers a relaxing spot where you can sit and hear the sounds of nature all around you?

Perhaps you are more of a Tuscan style girl and the idea of a pergola with ivy heavily entwined all over it, and a sparkling chandler dangling gorgeously from the center of it makes your heart skip a beat?

Today I am asking you about your dream home; however, when I ask you this, I am not talking about the style, color, or even the neighborhood of the house you long for. I am speaking of something much deeper and much more important. I am talking about your home, not your house.

Most of us have heard the childhood song; **The Wise Man Built His House upon the Rock.** In this song we see a wise man and a foolish man. The wise man built his house upon a rock and the foolish man built his house in the sand. We also know that when the storm comes, the house on the rock stood firm, while the house in the sand tumbles down. So let me ask you, how are you building your dream house? Are you building it upon the Rock, our Lord Jesus Christ; or are you building your home on the sand with everything the world has to offer?

What tools are you using to build your dream home?

Proverbs 14:1 says that *"Every WISE woman buildeth her house: but the foolish plucketh it down with her hands."*

The Bible is our guidebook and all throughout the Scriptures it shows us how we can build a secure home with a firm foundation. The Word of God also shows us what tools are most needed in building a solid structure.
In a society where the average Christian marriage last 5-7 years (at best) and couples now take the easy way out, I need advice on how to stay in for the long haul. There is simply no way I can do it on my own. As a wife and mommy of a four year old boy, I yearn for instructions

and guidance in marriage and motherhood!!

So to get started, I need a plan. I need a blueprint. I need to know what I'm going after and the goals I desire for my dream home. Everyone's dreams and goals for their home may look a little different, and that is perfectly fine. No two homes are exactly alike. Paint colors, décor style, floor plans, and personal preferences always make homes different, even if they have the same blueprint. My goals will look different than your goals and that's okay. The important fact to remember is to set goals and dreams for your home. Here are a few of mine.

1. I want my home to be a peaceful, relaxing, oasis, a safe refuge, and a little piece of Heaven here on earth. I don't want it to be a war zone with strife and conflict.

2. I want it to be a fun environment, a place where we laugh, play, and enjoy life, an area where we can be ourselves and feel comfortable. Whether it's staying in our pajamas all day on rainy days or the weekends, or going without makeup! (Whoop whoop!) I desire for it to be a location where we can gather together and enjoy life, and not feel judged.

3. I want God to be real in our home. I long for Him to be the center of my house. I want a relationship with God

that is so evident it inspires my family to get closer to God. I want Bible reading, prayer time, ministry work, and family devotions to be more than just a priority, but to be a passion! I strive for our family to have a walk with God that is so real it radiates in our neighborhood. I want my family, friends, and neighbors to feel the presence of God in our home.

Since I know what style of a home I am trying to build, let's think about the tools I will need in my toolbox. Why my toolbox and not my husband's? I'm so glad you asked! Notice the first part of the verse I just mentioned in Proverbs 14:1, *"Every wise woman buildeth her house..."* The responsibility is put upon the woman! You see ladies; we set the mood in our homes. We create the atmosphere in which we want to live. We know the old saying, *"If Momma ain't happy, ain't nobody happy."* Well, it's true! We are the keepers of the home, we are the mood setters, and we are the home builders.

So, let's look in our cute little pink toolbag and pick a few of the important tools we will need. My toolbox and tools might be a different color than yours, but that is not what's important. The important truth to remember is to pick up your tools and start building. A happy, peaceful, godly home is not constructed on accident, but with a well-thought-out, prepared plan.

So here is a list of my most needed tools:

Wisdom

Proverbs 9:1a *"Wisdom hath builded her house..."*

Proverbs 24:3a *"Through wisdom is a house builded..."*

Proverbs 14:1a *"Every wise woman buildeth her house..."*

I believe wisdom is the most important tool that each of us need. We need wisdom in our marriage, raising our children, running the home, staying organized, keeping a budget, multi-tasking, staying involved in church, taking care of ourselves, preparing healthy meals, carpooling kids, extra-curricular activities, encouraging others, helping our loved ones succeed, making time for our husbands, working a part time or full time job, and keeping our relationship with God personal and real. Yes, we need wisdom! We need it everyday and lots of it! Amen?

Trust

Proverbs 31:11 *"The heart of her husband doth safely trust in her..."*

Without trust it is hard to truly love and invest in

someone. I do not feel safe around people I do not trust, nor do I let my guard down around them. Home should be the safest place for a family, not a place to feel guarded or on the defense. I want my husband to safely trust in me with our home, our son, our money, and our future.

Kindness

Proverbs 31:26 *"She openeth her mouth with wisdom; and in her tongue is the law of kindness."*

We need to be just as kind to our family members as we are to our church families, co-workers, neighbors, and the general public. Kindness starts with our mouths, our words, and our speech. Hard one, I know! Sometimes it's so much easier to open our mouth with sarcasm than with kindness, but a home filled with kindness starts with a kind momma and a kind, graceful, gentle mouth.

Forgiveness

Ephesians 4:31-32 *"Let all bitterness, and wrath, and anger, and clamour, and evil speaking, be put away from you, with all malice: And be ye kind one to another, tender hearted, forgiving one another, even as God for Christ's sake hath forgiven you."*

Unfortunately, holding on to hurt never stops there, if you do not forgive, it becomes the breeding ground for all these other nasty, yucky sins to sneak in for the attack. No one sets out to be a bitter, wrathful, angry person; yet, when you hold on to unforgiveness and do not give forgiveness where it is due, then that is what you will became, BITTER!!!! That is not my prediction that is God's promise. I do not want any of these traits in my home. So, to prevent any of these from sneaking into my home, I must forgive. Forgiveness is a commandment from God. It is not an easy one, but it is a possible one with His strength!!! Do not let the little things become big things and don't let unforgiveness destroy your home.

A Sense of Humor

Proverbs 17:22a *"A merry heart doeth good like a medicine..."*

No amount of money can buy a happy home. You can have all the money in the world, the biggest house, and the newest cars; but if you can not enjoy life and laugh, it's all a waste. My husband has the corniest, driest sense of humor and I love it. I'm very task-oriented and could go all day without so much as a giggle. But thank goodness, my silly husband is very much the opposite and very much a goofball. He balances me out so well. My son also loves to laugh, and has the most contagious giggle. His enthusiasm for fun makes me stop and remember that I need to slow down and laugh more. With these two, I'm slowly learning to laugh at myself and my mistakes, as well as bloopers around the home. A home full of laughter is a happy home!!!

Hard Work and Patience

Proverbs 31:25 *"Strength and honor are her clothing; and she shall rejoice in time to come."*

All throughout Proverbs 31 we see how the virtuous woman was a hard, diligent worker. She was balanced and well skilled. She was selfless and disciplined. She took time to invest in every member of her household, and with persistence she made a house into a home. She may not have seen the fruits of her labors for many years. But the day her children called her blessed, I'm sure it was worth it all! Work hard, be patient, and leave the results up to God.

A Walk with God

We can not do this alone. If we were truly on the verge of building a home, we would hire a trained, skilled, professional contractor; one with a favorable reputation and lots of experience. Well, ladies, wives, mothers, and grandmothers use the Original Contractor. That's what He is here for. He wants us to come to Him,

He wants to help. He has the Master Plan. He wrote it and knows it pretty well. He has been in the "Home Building" business for a very long time. Glean from His expertise and experience. He has a pretty good success rate!!!

Let's remember a well built, solid house is not built with sloppy carelessness, by chance, or accident; but it's built with a well thought out plan, with preparation, and time. So with the Contractor, the Plan, the right tools and supplies we are well on our way to building our Dream Home. It will not happen over night. Nope, we all wished it worked that way. We must be diligent, we must plan, we must pray, and we must build. Because a lady that wants to sparkle and shine for God must first start in the home! Dream big and be a home builder!

Chapter Fifteen

The Quest for Peace

Peace

It's the one thing everyone searches for.

It's the one thing money can't buy.

It's what most people spend a lifetime trying to achieve and hold on to, and sadly, it's the one thing most people live without.

It's something that some people have spent hundreds and thousands of dollars hoping to obtain.

It's what everyone secretly wants and pretends to have.

It's no respecter of persons.

It's what puts the rich man and the beggar on common ground.

What is peace anyway?

Why does everyone want it?

Why is it so hard to find?

Is it possible to have peace?

Where can I find it?

Peace

It's what helps you sleep at night.

It's the calmness and quietness in your life.

It's the exact opposite of worry, fear, a troubled heart, and stress.

It's a softness, a state of mind, and a soothing tranquility.

We all desire peace because we all too often feel the pressures of this hectic, stressful, busy, loud, noisy, and sometimes scary world. Unfortunately, we too often look in all the wrong places to find peace. So is it even possible in this stressful, less than peaceful life to find peace, let alone hold on to it? The Bible tells us in Psalms 34:14b to *"....seek peace, and pursue it."* God tells us to seek for it and pursue it; He would never tell us to do something if it were not possible.

Peace is like a treasure and God has given us the treasure map with the exact details on where and how to find it. However, the devil also has a treasure map and a fake treasure chest. His map is full of detours and lies. He does not want you to find the real treasure and will keep you as far from it as possible. Let's take a quick look at a few of his fake treasures.

* Riches
* Material Substance
* The Perfect Body
* Popularity and Fame

* A Successful Career
* Achieving Perfection
* Drugs and Alcohol
* Well-behaved children
* A more attentive husband
* More followers on social media

While most of these are harmless and innocent, when they become an obsession or the destination for peace, they become nothing more than a fake treasure. None of these items can bring peace and contentment. Oh, they may offer a temporary satisfaction but not a lifetime of peace. If peace does not come through achieving perfection, then where does it come from? Where can we find it? Experts may say that more sleep, drinking more water, exercising more, or maintaining a healthier diet can help us have a peaceful life. While I am for all these things and I try to apply these to my life daily, they are not the answer. Like I mentioned earlier, some people have paid hundreds, even thousands of dollars and have tried all these options, just to find temporary contentment.

So, what is the answer, and how does a lady that desires to sparkle and shine for God obtain and retain that peace? Since the Bible is God's Map on how to get to the treasure, let's go there and see what it says.

John 14: 27 *" Peace I leave with you, my peace I give unto you: not as the world giveth, give I unto you. Let not your heart be troubled, neither let it be afraid."*

God does not give peace in the way that the world offers peace. The world fills our head with lies telling us to be rich, have things, be beautiful and perfect, be a successful career person and if that doesn't work, party it up and drink your worries away. We are surrounded by these lies on TV and in magazines. But God softly reminds us, *"...my peace I give unto you."*

John 16:20 *"These things I have spoken unto you, that in me ye might have peace, In the world ye shall have tribulation: but be of good cheer; I have overcome the world."*

Philippians 4:7 *"And the peace of God, which passeth all understanding, shall keep your hearts and minds through Christ Jesus."*

Did you see the answer?
Jesus!
Jesus, is the answer!

Jesus has always been the answer, and will always be the answer!

Isaiah says it beautifully in Isaiah 26: 3-4 " *Thou wilt keep him in perfect peace, whose mind is stayed on thee (Jesus): because he trusteth in thee (Jesus). Trust ye in the Lord for ever: for in the Lord JEHOVAH is everlasting strength.*" Then later in chapter 41:10 God says, "*Fear thou not; for I am with thee: be not dismayed; for I am thy God; I will strengthen thee; yea, I will help thee; yea, I will uphold thee with the right hand of my righteousness.*" God does not leave us stranded and without hope. He wants to help us live a victorious life with peace, courage, and strength. But it has to be His way.

Matthew 7:7-8 "*Ask, and it shall be given you; seek, and ye shall find; knock , and it shall be opened unto you: For every one that asketh receiveth; and he that seeketh findeth; and to him that knocketh it shall be opened.*"

Plain and simple, God wants you to ask Him and He desires for you to seek Him. Peace can be obtained and it can be retained, but it's only through Jesus. Hollywood has shown us time after time that riches, fame, nice things, beauty, and success can not bring true peace. So why not give God's way a try?

Maybe you don't know where to start, let me help you. Proverbs 3:1-2 the Bible says, *"My son, forget not my law but let thine heart keep my commandments: For length of days and long life, and peace, shall they add to thee."*

1. Start with Jesus

Be honest with yourself and be honest with God. You need it, and He is the one who has it, simply ask Him for peace.

2. Open your Bible and read His Words

You must go to Him daily and spend time with Him. You can not tap into His resources if you never spend time in His Word. Go to the Treasure Map.

3. Look for verses on peace and memorize them

Put verses up around your house to help you meditate on His promises. Memorize the ones that truly speak to your heart and when you are struggling, let that verse remind you of His love and mercy.

4. Turn over all your cares, worries, stress, frustrations, and doubts to Him

Do not try to carry the burden alone. In fact, do not carry the burden at all. Give it to God! No, scratch that, cast it, toss it, chunk it, throw it, whatever you have to do; just give it to Him.

1 Peter 5:7

"Casting all your cares upon Him for He careth for you."

5. Learn the Fruits of the Spirit and apply them to your life

Galatians 5:22-23 *"But the fruit of the Spirit is love, joy, **PEACE**, longsuffering, gentleness, goodness, faith, meekness, temperance…"*

6. Trust Him

Now, it's simply time to put your trust in Him. Is God big enough to take the hurt, the stress, the frustration, and the doubt out of your heart and replace it with peace? Is your God worthy of your trust? Is He big enough and mighty enough to carry the load for you?

7. Take His sweet gift

Ladies, God has given you the Map with a big X to

mark the spot. He wants you to be successful in this quest for peace. He desires for you to find the treasure, But He can not force it upon you just like I can not make you take the steps, I can only hand you the Map. It's up to you to find the treasure and accept the precious gift of His promises.

Romans 15:13
"Now the God of hope fill you with all joy and peace in believing that ye may abound in hope, through the power of the Holy Ghost."

I hope today, if you are drowning in stress, hurt, frustration, fear, anxiety, trouble, or anger; you will lay it all at the feet of Jesus and pick up His free gift of peace. Remember, He knows your name, He knows your heart, and He knows your hurt, and He wants to help! Let's show the world that we can live differently and we can choose to live a life with peace. Yes, we will continue to live in a world full of fear, hurt, and disappointments, but we can choose to live in faith, assurance, and peace. Let's sparkle and shine for Him in a life lived in beautiful peace.

Chapter Sixteen

Don't Shoot One of Your Own

Today, I write with a heavy heart. A heart that is broken, saddened, and appalled at how cruel and hateful Christians can be in the name of the Lord. One of my closest friends and I were talking today about one of our mutual friends. This friend is a dear sister in Christ and a pastor's wife. She recently went through a tragic time in her life with the loss of a baby, and then a very short time later, the unexpected passing of her mother. During this very critical time of horrific sorrow, her husband, family, and ministry came under fire and they were attacked. They were criticized, and had many people that they loved and respected simply turn their backs on them and walk away!

When they needed love, it was not offered. When they needed a friend, no one was there. When they could have used simple encouragement, it was replaced with gossip and shunning. And sadly, a short time later they left the ministry.

I can't help but shake my head out of frustration and wonder how is this Christ-like? No matter how much you disagree with someone or how bad of a mistake they have made, don't shoot them… HELP THEM!

This is a very tender subject for me because, I too was hurt by people I admired, respected, and loved. It took years to heal, recover, and get rid of the bitterness that I had allowed to take over. For a few years, I struggled with the lies of the devil to just throw in the towel and quit. But the love of God, and the faithful encouragement from family, and some very amazing Christian friends kept me from making that great mistake. It was a hard painful road to go down, but now I can see how even a painful experience can be used for the glory of God if we allow it. No doubt, I wouldn't be so sensitive and aware of the scrutiny and cruelty of Christians, had I not personally experienced it.

I'm not sharing this to seem like a pathetic victim. God knows me and all the mistakes I have made. I do not come to you as a blameless Christian or a perfect person. I come to you as a forgiven child of God with a heart that hurts for hurt people. Yes, I have unnecessarily judged people, I have participated in hurtful gossip, and my words and actions have hurt people. There are situations in my life I honestly wish I could go back and completely redo with mercy, love, and grace. This may be why God allowed me to go through this hurtful time, so that He could open my eyes to the damage that criticism can cause. Personally being on the receiving end of gossip allows you a much better perspective of what it feels like. It also allows you to be much more aware of the hurt caused by "judgy" Christians. So here are just a few thoughts on this:

If you are the one who has been hurt:
1. Keep your eyes on God and not the situation.
2. Learn to forgive.
3. Walk away from the attacker and walk to God.
4. Cling to God.
5. Allow time to heal.
6. Do not become bitter.
7. Trust in God, not in religion or man.
8. Learn to forgive, forgive, and forgive.
9. Repeat all the above steps.

If you are the Christian who has judged and hurt others, then please remember:
1. You are not the Ultimate Judge.
2. Don't let your pride or your religious beliefs hinder you from loving people like God loves them.
3. Treat others how you would want to be treated, or how

you would want your family to be treated.

4. Love them like Jesus loves them.

5. Forgive them.

6. Pray for them

7. Stay humble.

8. Let God use you to help them and restore them.

9. Don't walk away from them!

I absolutely love the verses in Galatians 6:1-3 *"Brethren, if a man be overtaken in a fault, ye which are spiritual, restore such an one in the spirit of meekness; considering thyself, lest thou also be tempted.*
Bear ye one another's burdens, and so fulfill the law of Christ. For if a man think himself to be something, when he is nothing, he deceiveth himself." When a Christian brother or sister has fallen, it is our duty to restore them, to carry their burden, and to fulfill the law of God. No, we do not sweep it under the rug or pretend it never happened, but we certainly should not be part of the rumor mill! We should use this as a golden opportunity to fulfill one of the greatest commandments in the Bible. Love one another. John 15:12a *"This is my commandment that ye love one another."* Not destroy, denounce, gossip, hate, shun, or turn your back on them.

Let's remember that before we take it upon

ourselves to expose another Christian's sins, we must first evaluate our own life. Matthew 7:1-5 *"Judge not, that ye be not judged. For with what judgment ye judge, ye shall be judged: and with what measure ye mete, it shall be measured to you again. And why beholdest thou the mote that is in thy brother's eye, but considerest not the beam that is in thine own eye? Or how wilt thou say to thy brother, Let me pull out the mote out of thine eye; and behold, a beam, is in thine own eye? Thou hypocrite, first cast out the beam out of thine own eye; and then shalt thou see clearly to cast out the mote out of thy brother's eye."*

You may argue that it is your job to warn the flock against heretics and wolves in sheep clothing. Although I totally believe you need wisdom, discernment, and discretion in handling these situations, I believe there is a Biblical way to argue, disagree, and a way to take a stand. However, I'm not talking about a heretic; I'm talking about your friend! I'm not talking about doctrinal issues, I'm talking about your personal preferences, standards, and convictions and the way you handle disagreements and the difference of opinions. How do you treat your brothers and sisters in Christ when they no longer think exactly like you do or they have made mistakes, or even fallen into sin? Do you stand by your friends when they no longer run in the same circle that you do? Do you continue to love them the way Jesus loves them, or do you shun them and walk away?

Let me challenge each of us, the next time we hear of a brother or sister in Christ who is hurting, sinned, or has made a terrible mistake; let's ask ourselves, *"What can I do to help?"*

    * Can I add them to my daily prayer list?
    * Can I encouragement them?
    * Can I keep my mouth shut to the gossip?
    * Can I be a friend to my friend?
    * Can I love them the way Christ loves them?
    * Can I agree to disagree?

None of us are perfect, sinless, or guiltless. We have all made mistakes but have found grace and mercy at the feet of Jesus. I come to you as an imperfect Christian who is genuinely striving to please God. I desire to love people like Jesus loves them and show them kindness the way Jesus shows kindness. If we could really grasp the definition of love, and loving people like Jesus loves them, our whole life, ministry, and the way we treat people would change. My plea to all of us is to remember that as Christians, we will not all see eye to eye. There will be things we will disagree on and stands that we will take that are different. But as a Christian, we must quit fighting each other and start fighting the true enemy! We are on the same team. We shouldn't be shooting each other. We are at war with the devil, not one another. Satan is the one we should be after. He is out to destroy homes, churches, friendships, ministries, and families. Let's quit helping him and stop fighting on his team. Let's all get back on God's team, rally around each other, pray for one another, and love one another. Let's protect each other and have each other's backs. We need each other as we battle against the true enemy. The cause of Christ is too great to do alone. Let's not walk away from brothers and sisters we don't agree with! Let's sparkle and shine as we pick up the fallen, reach out, and restore them. Our light will only be affective when we quit looking at everyone else's light. It's not our job to judge their light or blow it out. We can never shine a light to the world if we are trying to blow everyone else's light out. Remember to love them like Jesus loves them. *"People are In Need Of Kindness"* whether you agree with them or not.

And a happy little update on that sweet, precious, broken family that was attacked and eventually walked away from the ministry. They were soon blessed with a baby boy and are now currently serving God full-time in a different location. Praise God! He mends the broken hearted, heals the wounded, and restores the discouraged. Our God is an awesome God.

Chapter Seventeen

The Peacemaker

My all-time favorite Bible story is in II Samuel 25. It is the story of Abigail and how she stands as a mediator between David and her wicked husband, Nabal. In this incredible story, we see how the selfish, evil Nabal has refused a simple request for food made by David. We then see David's pride and anger hastily make the wrong decision for revenge. David did not pray about the situation, neither did he seek counsel. Instead he reacted quickly and allowed his anger to block his better judgment. He gave the orders and planned to kill everyone in the house of Nabal. When word got to Abigail that David and his men were coming, she immediately took action. She did not run from her horrible circumstances and the stressful conflict, in fact, she faced it head on. We read on to see how Abigail prepares a massive amount of food for David and his men. She personally meets David, humbles herself to him, encourages him, takes all the responsibility, and then pleads with him to change his mind. Unbelievable!!

Honestly, had this been me, I would have probably ran for the hills, or at the very least begged David to spare my life and then have his way with that selfish, evil horrible Nabal. But not Abigail, she was a peacemaker. She put her own life in danger in order to prevent a terrible manslaughter from happening. She protected hundreds of lives that day and also stopped David from later on having a guilty conscience and innocent blood on his hands.

There are so many lessons to be learned here and all throughout the Bible about being a peacemaker. Fortunately, most of us will never have to seek for peace at such a large magnitude as Abigail did. But we can still apply this in our everyday lives. How can you be a peacemaker? How can you be a godly mediator? How well do you handle confrontation, and how wisely do you stand up to conflict? Ouch, this hurts! This is not an easy lesson, and honestly it seems quite impossible. But with the help of our Lord and Savior, nothing is impossible. So, let's look at a few lessons or challenges that we can obtain from this precious peacemaker named Abigail.

1. A peacemaker's entire goal and focus is to create peace in the midst of chaos

Abigail knew what she had to do. She did not run

from the problem, she did not ignore the issue, she spared no expense, she did not take any short cuts, and she did not send anyone else to resolve the problem. Her objective was to peacefully rectify a matter, and she did not stop until she achieved her goal. Many times we want to run, ignore, take shortcuts, or dump the problem on someone else. But let's strive to create peace, whether it's with our family, our church, job, children, friends, neighbors, or with someone who has been offended. Let's make an effort to peacefully live, serve, work, and do life with others. It's easy in this busy society to just "write people off", or ignore the issue. Most of us would say we just don't have time for that kind of drama. But as Christian ladies, let's rise above the normal reaction, and let's make an attempt to create peace around us. There will be situations you will not be able to change or make better, but if you have honestly, sincerely, and wisely done everything in your power to offer peace, then you must leave the results up to God.

2. A peacemaker stands as a mediator drawing people back together

Abigail stood as a mediator between David and Nabal. She made a very selfless decision and put her own life in harm's way, and as a result saved hundreds of lives. She did not stand before David and point fingers at anyone. She did not add fuel to the fire by telling David how horrible Nabal was. She did not cause more drama or frustration to the situation. She used her words and actions wisely, defused the situation, and put the fire out. As Christians, we are given many opportunities to be a mediator. How do we choose to use these opportunities? Do we stir the pot? Add fuel to the fire? Create more drama and frustration? When your friend comes to you about something hurtful that someone said, or a situation that was mishandled, do you use this opportunity to be a peacemaker and defuse the situation, or do you add more drama and fuel to the fire? It's easy to give our two cents and our own opinion, but we are called to be different. We are called to create peace. We need to prayerfully consider wise, godly words and do our best to encourage the hurt friend without adding more frustration.

Man, do I wish I had this nailed down and never struggled with this topic. No, I have not perfected this, but boy, do I honestly want to. My desire is to be a peacemaker. I know I can improve and so can you. We can all strive to grow and do better. Don't choose to ignore this point just because you think it's hard, impossible, or pointless! Choose to be a peacemaker. Even if you struggle and fail, try again and ask God to help you. This is a wonderful way to sparkle and shine!

Proverbs 26:10 *"Where no wood is, there the fire goeth out: so where there is no talebearer, the strife ceaseth."*

3. A peacemaker will humbly encourage the offended

Notice that Abigail immediately bowed herself to David when she met him. She took all responsibility and did not defend herself. Wow! This is such a challenge. It is a natural human reaction to defend ourselves. No one wants to be falsely accused, or be held responsible for the wrong doings of others. But we see that Abigail did. She made no excuses, she just humbled herself. She offered David a peace offering, encouraged him, and she took full responsibility. There was no room for pride or her own personal agenda. I love that her humbled attitude and her encouraging words changed the outcome of the whole situation. The fate of her entire household was completely turned around because of her wise words and her humble actions.

How do your words help a situation? Do you choose peaceful words to inspire, challenge, encourage, and convict others, or do you allow your pride and personal agenda to get involved? Let's choose peace!

4. A peacemaker will handle confrontations and conflict wisely

This is the absolute hardest lesson for me. I'm more of a hit the hills running or stick my head in the sand kind of girl. Those who know me, know this is 100% truth. I hate confrontation, I despise conflicts, and I would rather ignore the problem than to face it head on. But we see in this story how Abigail wisely faces the problem. She neither ran away nor did she go into attack mode. She carefully approached the situation, and wisely faced it head on.

May we as Christian ladies strive to handle our issues like Abigail. Let's not be an ostrich with our heads in the sand or as a pitbull attacking everyone in our paths. May we choose to seek God and His unlimited resources when we have to confront those hard, difficult circumstances that we dread! As Christians, everything we do reflects Christ. We either bring honor or reproach to His name. It's not easy being a peacemaker, and sometimes it may even seem like it's not worth the effort. But may we truly strive to be a light that sparkles and shines for the glory of God. In this modern, new-age society where drama, conflict, sarcasm, brutal honesty, and personal agenda is totally acceptable, may we choose to be an Abigail and stand for humility, meekness, encouraging words, wisdom, and peacemaking.

"Blessed are the peacemakers: for they shall be called the children of God." Matthew 5:9

Chapter Eighteen

A Humbled Heart

I truly believe one of the most effective ways to sparkle and shine and reach others for Christ, is to be a humble, sincere child of God. The world is not looking for a hot shot with all the answers; and they do not need someone who is full of themselves. They need someone who is real, honest, and humbly pointing them to the cross. The Christian walk is not about anything we have done, conquered, built, or succeeded in. It's all about what God has done for us and through us. God graciously allows us to serve Him and do a work for Him. We may see amazing victories and outstanding results, but we must stay humble and remember to give God all the glory. We must have a humble heart and not allow pride and our ego to get in the way. It is God and God alone that exalts us and our ministries, but it is not so we can see fame, glory, or fortune, it is so we can reach more people for Christ and give God all the praise and honor. So, as we are doing a work for God and following our dreams, or seeing a huge goal finally coming true, here are a few pointers that God has shown me time and time again, and I would like to share them with you.

1. Humble yourself

"Humble yourselves therefore under the mighty hand of God, that he may exalt you in due time." I Peter 5:6
Maybe you have a dream or a desire in your heart that you don't know how to accomplish. Humble yourself to God, lay that dream down at His feet, and give it to Him. It's simply amazing what can be accomplished if it is done in His strength, and through His power. There is nothing too big or too small for God. More than likely He is the one who placed that dream in your heart and He is simply waiting for you to give it back to Him.
"Delight thyself also in the Lord; and he shall give thee the desires of thine heart. Commit thy way unto the Lord; trust also in Him; and he shall bring it to pass. And he shall bring forth thy righteousness as the light..."
Psalm 37:4-6a

We can trust God with our desires and our dreams. But we must first commit them to the Lord and trust in Him. Does this verse mean that God will give us every want and every desire we have. Um, No!! I know there are popular preachers that preach of a prosperity gospel and that if you serve God you will drive a Porsche and life will always be wonderful. As nice as that would be, that is not what this verse is saying. I believe that God places certain desires and dreams in our hearts, dreams that seem impossible and unattainable, just so we will commit them back to Him and accomplish them through His strength. Why? So He alone can get all the Glory.

Perhaps your dream is a calling in the ministry, reaching your family for Christ, a certain career, writing a book, starting a new ministry in church. Maybe your desire is more personal and you want to lose weight, volunteer in the community, get out of debt, learn an instrument, or go back to school and get a degree. Whatever your dream and desire is, give it to God, trust Him, and then follow His direction.

"Trust in the Lord with all thine heart; and lean not unto thine own understanding. In all thy ways acknowledge him, and he shall direct thy path." Proverbs 3:5-6

While studying the life of Abigail in the previous chapter, I was amazed at her humble spirit. She humbled herself to David and was able to victoriously save hundreds of lives. And then she goes home and does not boast about her tremendous triumph. She could have gone home to her foolish husband and smeared this great victory all in his smug face. She could have tooted her own horn for everyone in the house to hear, but that was not her way. She wisely waited for the right opportunity to relate the details to her husband. She was one wise, humble lady of God. And later in the story, we see how God delivers her from her wicked husband, rescues her from a miserable marriage, and then exalts her to become the wife of David. Such a pretty amazing ending!

2. Serve others and love them

Remember that while you are doing a work for God or chasing after a dream, the main purpose is to love and invest in others along the way. The ultimate goal is not to accomplish dreams just to become a success, or build a big ministry, a popular name, or an enormous empire. The ultimate goal is the reach others for Christ. Don't get so focused on the task at hand that you forget to serve, love, and invest in those around you. What a shame it would be to stand before the King of Kings on the Day of Judgment having accomplished all your dreams, yet failing to reach others. On that day, I pray there will be others along beside me that I have reached, loved, touched, and invested in.

Yes, follow your calling, work hard, and accomplish those dreams; but be aware of others and invest in the lives of the people God has put in front of you.

3. Do the work and be faithful

There will be days that the work will seem impossible, frustrating, boring, tedious, pointless, and worthless; but if you know that it is what you have been called to do, then keep on going. You may find yourself burned out and weary, but remember, the amazing promise in Galatians 6:9 *"And let us not be weary in well doing; for in due season we shall reap, if we faint not."* Don't give up, keep on going. Don't faint be faithful. One of my elementary teachers recently reached out to me and shared that she was going on fifty years as the piano player at her church and as a Sunday school teacher. Fifty years! Friends, let's be faithful to the ministry God has placed us in.

4. Leave the results up to God

Obviously, anytime you are following your dreams or doing a work for the Lord, you desire to be a success. No one starts up a new work with the intentions of being a failure. No, you dream big, work hard, and desire to see amazing results. But we must remember, the results are not up to us, they are up to God. We must do our part and do everything we can possibly do, then we must step aside and let God be God. I think this step is so hard for most of us control freaks. It's hard for us to let go and let God. We want to hold on to the reins, but it is not our place. I Corinthians 3:6 reminds us that *"God gives the increase."* Be faithful to the work and leave the results up to God. Remember, it's our job to obey; we will receive our true rewards in Heaven. Don't get distracted by numbers or results. God does not measure success the same way we measure it. His ways are not our ways! And He certainly does not think the way we think. We get caught up in earthly rewards when God values Heavenly rewards.

5. Give God the Glory

No matter how big or how small the victory may be, remember to give God the glory. Stay humble and give praise where praise is due. He alone is worthy of our honor, our praise, and our worship. Let's keep it all about Him. I Timothy 1:17 *"Now to the King eternal, immortal, invisible, the only God, be honor and glory forever and ever. Amen."*

There is no telling what God can do through you, your dreams, and your ministry if you are humbly obedient to him, faithfully working hard, leaving the results up to Him, and giving Him the glory. God wants to use you, don't be scared to dream big and go for it.

I Corinthians 2:9 *"But as it is written, eye hath not seen, nor ear heard, neither have entered into the heart of man, the things which God hath prepared for them th' love him."*

Chapter Nineteen

Shine Passionately Where You Are

It's easy to think that your little light will never make an impact on the world; therefore it is insignificant and shining your light isn't even worth the effort. Dear sister, look up into the heavens and look at all the power and all the magnificent splendor of all the stars. They shine as a mighty army twinkling for the glory of God; and we can do the same. Please remember that someone needs your light and someone is depending on you. Shine where you are and shine passionately. Don't compare your light to anyone else's light. We all have our place in this world, and there is plenty of room for all of us. Let's think about the sun, moon, and the stars. I seriously doubt the stars get jealous of the sun and all the attention it gets during the day. And I really don't think the sun get envious of the moon and the fact that it gets to hang out with all the stars at night. I'm pretty sure they just do their job, and do it faithfully. Why? Because they each have a very important job to do, and they just do it.

In Genesis 1:15, we see that God created two great lights, the greater one to rule the day and the lesser one to rule the night. Then we read on to see something interesting, *"He made the stars also."* He thought it was important enough to mention the stars too. Even though individually their light is pretty small in comparison to the Sun, they are a spectacular sight and a mighty force when they are all shining together.

Each one of these lights have a unique job designed for a special purpose. No matter the size of your light or the size of your ministry; shine knowing you were created for a unique job and you were designed for a special purpose. Bring passion back into your calling and sparkle and shine! Don't get sidetracked with who may have a bigger light, or a bigger realm of influence. Let's passionately shine in the place that we have been put.

Let's get passionate about our relationship with the Lord again. For many of us, we have made God a priority. And while making Him a priority is great, it can also be dangerous. Let's be careful not to make Him just part of our daily checklist. I have lots of priorities that I am not at all passionate about. I wash dishes, dust, sweep, do laundry and clean toilets. I do this out of duty and obligation, and I can promise you there is no passion involved in these task. If I'm not careful, I can put my Bible reading, daily devotions, prayer time, and Bible memory down on my daily checklist and see it as nothing more than a duty or an obligation. This might be why there is no passion in churches anymore. If there is no passion in our daily walk with God, then there will be no passion in our ministries and in our callings! Just remember, you become passionate about things you are invested in. You are invested in things that you love. You love things that have your heart. Don't make God just a priority, allow Him to become a passion. Get invested in the things of the Lord and give Him your heart.

If your light has either been burned out, or you have gotten sidetracked, then get back on track and allow God to rekindle your flame and burn for Him. Just imagine if we all served the Lord with a renewed spark and a fervent passion. Not just for a year or two, but for a lifetime. Whether we are serving alone or serving along side others, may we put our eyes on the Lord and remember that our labor is not in vain. Let's apply I Corinthians 15:58 back into our lives, *"Therefore, my beloved brethren, be ye steadfast, unmoveable, always abounding in the work of the Lord, forasmuch as ye know that your labour is not in vain in the Lord."* What we do for the Lord is not in vain! You may feel like you are not making a difference, but you are!

Imagine a Sunday school teacher that faithfully

teaches her class or the music minister that shows up for practice prepared and spirit filled. Imagine the children's church workers that eagerly teach on their assigned Sunday with an exciting Bible lesson. Think of the mother who prays endlessly for the salvation of her children and the business lady who is cheerful and helpful at work. The Christian life is not about who has a bigger light, it's about shining your light where you are, and reaching and investing in the ones God has put in your path. Might we all remember, it's not our light we are shining, it's the Lord's, and anything we do is all for the glory of God.

Now, look back up into the heavens, pick a star (or a satellite) and let that light be your constant reminder to serve faithfully and shine passionately for the Lord. Not because we have to, but because we get to!

Chapter Twenty

Awake Arise and Shine

Ladies, it's time. It's time to get up, go out, and let our lights shine. We were not given our lights so we could keep them to ourselves in the comfy-cozy, safe environment of our homes. God did not start a flame in our hearts so that that we could build a fire at home and enjoy it with just our families. Nope, He calls us to go out into the Highways and the Hedges, to the outcast, the destitute, to the poor, and to the weak. He challenges us to follow Him and share His Light with everyone we come in contact with. Whether it's at the grocery stores, the baseball fields, with the telemarketers blowing up our phones, or the waitress in the restaurant; we have been called to go out and share the light He has ignited in our hearts.

Ephesians 5:14
"Wherefore he saith, Awake thou that sleepest, and arise from the dead, and Christ shall give thee light."

Awaken

1. Wake up out of your slumber

We must wake up. We live in a very self-centered environment. There are hurt people all around us and yet we choose to live in our bubble where it's nice and safe. We go to church, sing our songs, get inspired by the preaching, minister to our own family and friends, stay in the comfortable walls of our homes and churches, and continue to live our daily lives. There must be a change! We must wake up and open our eyes to the needs of our community. We must get out of the comfort zone of our bubble and get our hands dirty serving others and loving God. Yes, it may be uncomfortable; it may inconvenience our schedules and it may even rattle our way of thinking! But we can not continue as we always have. We can not let our daily lives and routines stop us from reaching out to others. We can serve God everywhere we are, but we must WAKE UP and see where He is leading us.

2. Wake up to your calling

What has God called you to do? Where is God leading you to serve? What passion has He given you? What are your dreams and your goals? Wake up and discover what

His plan and purpose is for you. Life was never meant for you to live without God's plan, purpose, or passion burning in your soul. He has something so unique for you to do; but you must be willing to follow His leadership and His guidance. You must wake up to what God is calling you do to. If you do not know what your calling is, begin with praying and asking God to reveal it to you. Spend time with Him and seek His will. Go to your pastor and ask for his advice and counsel. Look for areas in your church to serve.

Perhaps you know what your calling is but for what ever reason, you have not followed through with it. May I encourage you to jump up and get busy? Ask yourself why you are not following Him in your calling. Is it laziness, fear, insecurities, self-doubt, shortcomings, or just plain disobedience? You have one chance to live this life, so please, live it well. There are no second chances, no do-overs, and no retakes. You get one shot, one chance, one opportunity. That's all we are all given. Life is but a vapor and soon it will pass. Serve Him while you can. Do not wait and wish you had. Don't live a life full of regrets, or "what ifs", and "had onlys". There are hundreds of excuses and reasons why you can't or why it might not be a good time; but please WAKE UP to your calling. You will never regret a life lived for God.

3. Wake up to your investments

Where your treasure is there will your heart be also. Where do you invest your time? How do you invest your money? Is your heart tender for the things of God? The only things that will last for eternity are the things we do for Him. Are you selfish with your time? Do you only make time for your little world and the people that live in it? Do you make time for Kingdom work, community outreach, work days at the church, revivals, conferences, ladies Bible studies, and mission projects? Or do you keep your time and your schedule selfishly rotating around your little world. Wake up dear sister and allow your little world to rotate around the work of the Lord. You can involve your family and your friends! Invest your time into your church, into serving God, into your community and allow God to use you.

Now, what about money? OUCH, this one hurts! Are you willing to dig deep and give even if it means you do without? Are you willing to write a check to a missionary, knowing it might mean you have to struggle a little with your own personal budget? Are you willing to pay for a stranger's groceries if God lays it upon your heart? Are you willing to open up your pocket book and give what's in there if God asks you to? It is not an easy topic and it's not an easy act of obedience. We work hard for our money and we want to keep it. But God wants our hearts and He desires our obedience. He knows if He can get our money and our time, He can have our hearts. Wake up and see where your investments are, this will show you where your heart is.

Arise

1. Get up

The hardest part of my day is not waking up, nope that comes pretty easily. Maybe it's due to a four year old jumping on my head! But, normally at the same time every day, my sleeping eyes began to leisurely open. I wake up pretty easy, so that is not the hardest part of my day. The hardest part of my day is getting up out of the bed. It's so warm and comfortable; it's very safe, snug, and secure. I have no desire to ruin my peaceful environment with the realities of a non-stop day. I don't really want to step out of my tranquil, restful, untroubled oasis and onto the cold, hard floor full of responsibilities.

No, I would much rather just stay put where I am happy, comfy, cozy, and safe. And I would dare say this is how many of us view God's calling on our lives. He has laid a dream deep in our hearts and it scares us to death. We are unsure of the future and the security it may offer. We are scared to get up and follow Him. We are comfortable, safe, secure, untroubled, and happy right where we are. We don't have control over the unknown and it looks scary and hard. So, we choose to lay back down in the bed and throw the blanket over our heads. No, No, No! Ladies, we can not live in fear. We have to get up. We have to get out of the boat (or the bed) and follow God. He may lead us to places we could have never dreamed, but we will never know if we do not GET UP! Are you willing to get uncomfortable for God? Are you willing to get out of the safety of your comfort zone and walk into uncharted territories? It may mean walking out of the walls of your church to start an outreach ministry. It may require you to sacrifice a peaceful, lazy Friday night at home, are you willing? Please, just get up and be willing to get out!

2. Get up and get moving

I love Acts 9. It just might be my second favorite story in the Bible, cause remember, I Samuel 25 is my favorite story! And Abigail is my Bible Hero, and I can't wait to meet her in Heaven! Oh, but back to Acts 9, it is a chapter that beautifully shows the power of God. It displays one of the most remarkable salvation transformations in history. In a previous chapter we saw how Saul was miraculously changed into Paul. We read how a Christ hater became a Christ follower. We also saw in that chapter how Paul was restored his sight, baptized, and filled with the Holy Ghost. Then in verse 20 we saw the verse, *"And straightway he preached Christ!"* He did not waste any time following God and getting busy with his new calling. Paul did not hesitate or negotiate his calling. He accepted it and obeyed it. Ladies, we must get up and get moving. We must take our callings seriously and move forward. We shouldn't hesitate or negotiate with God. We should humbly accept our calling and "straightway" take the plunge. Now, please don't get me wrong, some ministries take time to start, some dreams take years to accomplish, and some callings will take a period of training to prepare for. I'm not taking the importance away from God's timing. I'm trying to emphasize the importance of letting go of the excuses and taking that first step forward! Get up and get moving. If you need to prepare for your callings, then start there. If you need to take classes, read books, learn a new language, or recruit helpers for a new ministry, then get busy. Start by just starting. Do something. Whether it is the praying stage, the planning process, or the getting it started phase; get up and get moving in that direction. Crawl or take baby steps if you must, but just move from where you are right now and move forward. Get up and get moving.

3. Don't let difficulties or rejections stop you from moving forward

You may not have the support of others around you in your journey. You may feel insecure and rejected in this dream or calling. It may feel awkward and uncomfortable. But if you know that it is from God then keep on going and keep on moving forward. Take it one step at a time and one day at a time. Look for the doors that God is opening up around you and follow Him. Sometimes our dreams and our callings are not the way we envisioned them. The time line might be much differently than what we had hoped for. And that's okay. We don't think like God does so as long as our trust and our obedience is in Him; then our dreams and our callings are safe and secure in Him. Do what you're supposed to do; and leave the result up to Him.

In Acts 9: 20-29, we see the calling of Saul and how it started for him. He preached truth and he testified that Christ was the Son of God, but he was still rejected by believers and non-believers. However, that did not stop Paul. He could have gotten down and discouraged, but we see he kept going. God increased his ministry and Paul continued on in strength and boldness. He continued to follow God and did not let difficulties and rejections stop him from moving forward.

There will be bumps along the way, there will be detours and delays, but no matter what, we must never take our eyes off the destination. We must continue on the journey of our callings and continue to move. If it takes longer than we ever expected, or if it happens differently than we anticipated. Keep moving forward and keep following God. We are not responsible for the results; we are responsible for our obedience. So, let's not allow the difficulties and rejections discourage us or hinder us from moving forward. Let's allow those difficulties and those rejections to make us stronger and bolder in our calling, for the glory of God.

<u>Shine</u>

1. We must be different

As a Child of God, there must be something different about us. We need to be a ray of sunshine and a hope in this dark and depressing world. We must live our lives differently, choose our words wisely, and make our actions godly. We should be different in a positive way. Our difference should draw others to us, not away from us. A righteous life should be something that the world longs for, not despises. We should draw people to us, not away from us. We can not shove our beliefs hatefully down other people's throats! Let's lovingly and patiently reach others and guide them to Christ. But we must have something that they want. If we are no different than the lost world and we do not have anything to offer that's different, then why do they need what we have?

2. Get out of your safety bubble and spread your light

Who has God called you to shine and sparkle to? Who is it that He wants you to share your light with? Most of us are so comfortable in our little bubble that we fail to see the mission field all around us. It's at the grocery stores, the work place, it's out at the ball field, the hospitals, the homeless shelters, the jails, our neighborhoods, and at a community volunteer center. Where is God calling you? Look outside the windows of your home and outside the doors of your church and start spreading your light.

I remember an elderly lady, who was basically a shut-in, telling me she would pray every day for an opportunity to share God. She would eagerly wait for the phone to ring and would get so excited to find a telemarketer on the other end. She would patiently wait and respectfully listen to their annoying sales pitch, and then she would share the gospel with them. She eagerly awaited the daily arrival of the mailman, just so she could offer him words of encouragement and praise. She would give cold water bottles or hot coffee to the UPS man.

She prayed for opportunities, looked for them, and then took hold of the opportunity once it presented itself. We each have golden opportunities everyday if we choose to see them and take hold of them. Get out of your comfort zone and let your light shine. Be courageous with the Gospel.

3. Shine for the glory of God

To truly shine for the glory of God, we must shine for His glory and His alone. We are not called to shine our lights so that others will notice us, what we have done, or what we can accomplish. We are not shining our lights for opportunities, recognition, popularity, or fame. We can not go around shining a light with the hope of creating a name for ourselves or the intentions of building a larger ministry. We can not sparkle just so we can gain more followers on social media, accomplish fame, or make a fortune. No, most of the time to completely sparkle and shine we will not gain anything, we might actually lose friends, opportunities, and find ourselves without a large support group. As Christians, our ultimate goal should be to follow God and glorify Him in everything we do. Your name may never be written in neon lights but God knows your name and what you have done for Him. May we choose to follow

God and not fame, religion, or our own agenda. May we choose to shine, and shine bright for the King of Kings! He is the only one who is worthy of our praise, our worship, our obedience, and our service! May our lights shine for the glory of God.

Okay, so my brain is doing it again. I can't help it or stop it, it just unconsciously goes straight to children's songs. And right now I caught myself singing, **Rise and Shine**. You know it, so you might as well sing along with me.

> **So, rise and shine and give God the glory glory**
> **Rise and shine and give God the glory glory**
> **RISE and SHINE and (clap)**
> **Give God the glory glory**
> **Children of the Lord.**

We each have a light to shine. We have a dream to share, and a calling to live! Now, we must wake up, get up, and light up the darkness around us. So friends, sparkle and shine wherever you are and shine to the people God has called you to. We have been called to be a light. Will you go? Will you share your light?

"Wherefore he saith, Awake thou that sleepest, and arise from the dead, and Christ shall give thee light." Ephesians 5:14

Conclusion

In a society where Christians are looked upon with hate, distrust, and disgust; may you courageously let your light shine! Might you confidently let your light sparkle and shine as you show the world that Jesus loves them. Let's lovingly stand up for Jesus in a dark world. Let's boldly proclaim His name into the ears of the haters and unapologetically serve others. Might we love as Jesus loved (and loves). Give as Jesus gave. Serve as Jesus served. Sacrifice as Jesus sacrificed Are you willing to live a holy, righteous life like Jesus lived? Be a friend to the friendless, help the helpless, minister to others outside the church? Are you willing to be real, open, and honest?

Don't be scared to let your light shine. Don't be afraid of rejection or ridicule. Stand strong knowing we have freedom from fear. Psalm 27:1 *"The LORD is my light and salvation; whom shall I fear? The LORD is the strength of my life; of whom shall I be afraid?"* When we walk in the light of the Lord we can have the strength, the courage, and the boldness to shine radically for Him. God calls us to shine our light unto a darkened world. To shine, we must be different. And to be different, we must come out of the world and be separate. But don't confuse this with separating yourself entirely out of the world. Don't ever be so heavenly minded you can't do any earthly good. We should not act like the world, but we should try to reach the world.

So my question to you is; are you willing to let your light shine? Are you ready to be a radiant light for the Lord? Will you Sparkle and Shine in a Dark and Dreary World?

Proverbs 4:18

"But the path of the just is as the shining light, that shineth more and more unto the perfect day."

Made in the USA
Monee, IL
19 November 2021

82527461R00105